SEASONS OF GRACE

A Spiritual Companion to the Liturgical Year

WALTER KASPER

Paulist Press
New York / Mahwah, NJ

Cover image: Triptych created 1966/67 by Franz Drapeia. Photo by Herzi Pinki / Wikimedia Commons.
Cover and book design by Lynn Else

Library of Congress Cataloging-in-Publication Data is available upon request.

ISBN 978-0-8091-5395-4 (paperback)
ISBN 978-1-58768-568-2 (e-book)

Published by Paulist Press
997 Macarthur Boulevard
Mahwah, New Jersey 07430

www.paulistpress.com

Printed and bound in the
United States of America

CONTENTS

CONTENTS

Contents

CONTENTS

Contents

CONTENTS

Contents

TRANSLATOR'S NOTE

This volume is a companion to one published by Paulist Press in fall 2016: Walter Kasper's *Faith: Practices, Models, and Sources of the Spirit*. Together these two English texts contain almost all the material published in one long German volume that first appeared in 2009 to mark the twentieth anniversary of Kasper's ordination as a bishop. That volume received another, slightly expanded German edition in 2014.[1]

Most of the material published in both English volumes is made up of excerpts of homilies and pastoral talks given by Kasper between 1989 and 1999, when he was bishop of the German Catholic Diocese of Rottenburg-Stuttgart.

The 2016 English volume comprised eight chapters organized thematically around the topic of faith. This new volume finds its organization in the church's liturgical year. After an introductory chapter (first written by Kasper for the 2014 German volume) on the liturgical year, the bulk of this book is arranged according to the seasons of the church year—with successive chapters on Advent/Christmas, Ordinary Time, Lent, Easter, and Pentecost. The individual reflections are excerpts of homilies on lectionary readings for specific Sundays and feasts. The final two chapters (on "Living from

---

1 Walter Kasper, *Wer glaubt, zittert nicht: Ermutigung zum Glauben* (Freiburg: Verlag Herder, 2014). This text runs to 470 pages.

the Sacraments" and "Sacred Music—Church Music") form a bookend to the introductory chapter on the church year.

Laid out in this way, the book is intended as a companion for preachers and for those who wish to pray the church's lectionary readings for Sundays throughout the year.

This volume, *Seasons of Grace*, picks up on the theme of "lived faith" that echoes through all its texts. Kasper's preaching aims to address the difficulties that "lived faith" faces in our day. Those difficulties have many causes, one of which is our utilitarian market-driven secular culture that too often "subjugate[s] human beings to the rhythm of work" (5). This has left us in a "world turned tired and cold" (29), where we find ourselves living "thoughtlessly and without direction" (158).

But Kasper also thinks the institutional church itself can become a cause, when it lacks "the oil of the Holy Spirit": "Occasionally one has the impression that the 'gears' of the church itself are missing such oil. Instead of oil, there seems to be sand in the church's gears. This is why the gears grind, and the vehicle occasionally runs hot" (167).

We individual believers also contribute by failing to engage the depth of Scripture and of the tradition of faith: "Do we even know the wealth we have here, what treasures lie buried here? Are we aware that many criticize a tradition they do not really know any more?" (169). Kasper adds, "The real danger in our time does not come from those who oppose the church, but from our own indifference and apathy. Our self-satisfaction and inertia are the death of faith" (18).

The antidote that Kasper proposes to our situation is as straightforward as it is challenging: "We need the healing power of the gospel in this situation." We need "lived faith":

> Faith is the most worthwhile of all things. But we
> are only able to pass on...what we ourselves have

lived....We must allow the love, mercy, and salvation of our God to enter completely into us; we
must allow them to grow warmer and then burst
into flame in our own hearts and lives, if we want to
set them alight in others. (104)

Or, again: "[The Apostle Paul] says that the only thing
that counts is faith working through love. What could the true
fruit of faith be except love! Without love, all else amounts to
nothing" (140).

This theme of lived faith is arguably the central concern of Kasper's now sixty years of ordained ministry. (He
was ordained a priest for the German diocese of Rotten-
burg on April 6, 1957.) At his episcopal ordination, Kasper
chose words from Paul's Letter to the Ephesians (4:15) as his
motto: "doing the truth in love" (*Veritatem in caritate*). The
theme also echoes through Kasper's theology. While he was
still teaching full time in the theology faculty at Tübingen,
Kasper wrote the following about his concern for the church
of our day:

Today we are unfortunately bound to say that in the
souls of many believers the church is dying. These
believers still probably live *in* the church, but they
are less and less *living the church* and its faith....
[Yet] our situation contains the potential for a more
conscious and more personally implemented faith.[2]

Kasper's pastoral ministry and his theology are rooted in a
deep insight of the Christian tradition—namely, that faith and
love are so interdependent as to be impossible one without
the other. The Letter of James has it that "faith without works

2 Walter Kasper, *Theology and Church*, trans. Margaret Kohl (New York:
Crossroad, 1989), 141–42.

is…dead" (James 2:26). Aquinas and the Catholic theological tradition have distinguished "formed" and "unformed" faith: faith that does not open out into a life of love and generosity is "unformed" (*fides informata*), that is, essentially incomplete.[3] We may see ourselves as *having* faith, but we are not actually *living* our faith.

May the reflections of this volume help us in our own attempts to live our faith. May their arrangement according to the church's lectionary increase their usefulness to believers and preachers seeking lived faith day in and day out throughout the year. I remain very grateful to Paulist Press for the opportunity to translate Kasper's writing. As before, any errors in the translation are mine.

William McDonough
May 30, 2017

---

3 Thomas Aquinas is the classical source of this distinction. See his *Summa Theologiae* I-II. 113. 4; 114. 3; and 4.8.

CHAPTER ONE

THE CHURCH YEAR— ORDINARY TIME AND SEASONS OF GRACE

THE CHURCH YEAR: CRISIS AND REDISCOVERY OF A CULTURAL INHERITANCE

The church year or, as it is more formally called, the liturgical year has shaped our European culture over many centuries. Each week was marked by the distinction between Sundays and work days. Sundays were distinguished from the rest of the week by the general rest from work and the more or less common practice of going to church in Sunday dress. For centuries people's experience of the calendar year was through the rhythms of Christian holidays, particularly Advent, Christmas, Lent, and Easter, with the three days of the Sacred Triduum. At the Feast of Corpus Christi, the liturgy became a sacramental procession through town streets and squares. At the same time, the calendar year was marked by prominent saints' days, especially the

Marian feasts, the feasts of church patrons, and other local popular church festivals. All these festivals were embellished by popular piety and rich folk customs.

This culture of Sundays and feast days gave a rhythm and color to life. So, for centuries, the church was able to shape a religious folk culture that is now coming to an end as we more and more value and implement processes of inculturation. For the transition from an agrarian society that lived according to seasonal changes to a modern industrial society that subordinates everything to the laws of economy and efficiency has brought with it an altered rhythm that competes with the traditional rhythm of the church year. Sundays have become "the weekend," and holy days have become holidays. For many people, their yearly vacation has become the high point and most beautiful time of the year.

The declining number of churchgoers shows a diminishing interest of many Christians in the liturgical celebrations of the church year. The number of people with little or no interest in the Christian Sunday and Christian feast days continues to grow. Many cultural remnants of Christianity live on as a kind of cultural Christianity, but beneath the surface it is often difficult to find much Christian substance. In particular, much of what really was lived in village life threatens to become mere folklore.

And a new social and religious pluralism is entering into the mix. People of other cultural and religious traditions, especially Muslims, live among us as our neighbors. They rightly enjoy religious freedom, practicing their religion and bringing it to bear not only privately but also publicly. So the public observance of the Christian Sunday and feast days is often seen as a threat to social peace and called out-of-date.

Yet when the rhythm of the church year no longer gives a rhythm to daily life, then the monotonous succession of days, weeks, months, and years will be experienced simply as boredom, and festivals and celebrations will take on their own individualized forms. Such a gain in individual freedom has its downside. A new leisure market has arisen in which approaches to free time and celebration are widely controlled and marketed through advertising. What were once religious gatherings often become mere distractions; holiday rest often becomes vacation stress; holiday joy becomes only diversion. And while none of this is objectionable if it is kept in proportion, it often lacks existential and religious depth and brings people back empty to their everyday lives.

So, it is understandable that interest in folk piety, in pilgrimages and processions is rising again; it is also understandable that there is interest in renewed forms of cultures of religious festivals and of the Christian Sunday. More and more people are getting away for retreats and contemplative weekends or are looking for times of contemplation and rest in monasteries. The number of families or groups of families that organize themselves into house churches is growing, as is the number of spiritual communities. In opposition to dominant social trends, these are attempts at a more conscious participation in the seasons and life of the church year. And so it is worth our time to reflect anew on the meaning and shape of the liturgical year and to ask how we can live it with new energy.

THE RHYTHM OF SABBATH AS A HUMAN CULTURAL INHERITANCE

Our human cultural inheritance bears reconsideration. Religious festivals are an ancient human tradition. Human beings have always experienced time as fleeting. Days, weeks, months, and years fly by. What was vanishes, never to return. Already Heraclitus (535–475 BCE) said that one may not step twice into the same river, for neither the river nor the person is the same the second time around.[1] And so human beings have always searched for fixed points in the stream of time. Such points were found in the sun's movements and in the phases of the moon. The earth's orbit of the sun gives the rhythm of the seasons, especially the blossoming of nature in spring and the rich harvests of autumn. Both events were understood as signs of cyclic renewal; they were understood and celebrated as part of the divine cosmic life force.

The Bible took up the religious seasonal festivities of the ancient Eastern traditions and understood them anew. Especially in the psalms, the Bible praises the wonderful order of the world; it is familiar with the rhythm of days, weeks, and years; it understands this rhythm as the created image and reflection of God's glory (see Pss 8, 19, 104, 148, and others). But, for the Bible, the world in all its order, beauty, and magnificence is not itself divine and God does not arise from the cosmos and its order. For the Bible, the stars, sun, and moon, revered by some as divine, are only created realities, referred to almost dismissively as lamps to serve as signs for human beings of seasons, days, and years (see Gen 1:14).

Thus, the first book of the Bible can explain the creation of the world in the temporal order of six days, so that this week of the world's existence may culminate in the seventh day, a world-sabbath as it were. On this day, God rests from his work (Gen 2:3ff.) That does not mean that God became tired in creating the world and had to rest. Augustine said that God rests in himself, that God is God's own rest.[2] Human dignity certainly consists in our being able to rejoice in the world and to work in and with it, but it is our special blessing as human beings to participate in Sabbath. Through Sabbath, we humans may and should rise above the world, above work, and above all the unrest and instability of the world to partake in God's peace and rest (see Exod 20:8–11; 31:12–17; Deut 5:12–15).

The Sabbath is more than a day on which we do nothing in order to rest from the burden of work and strengthen ourselves to work again. Unlike our modern economic system, the Bible does not subjugate human beings to the rhythm of work. In the Bible, what governs life is not the rhythm of work but the rhythm of feasts and celebrations. The human being was not created as a workhorse or as a slave to work. We are created in freedom to rise above the demands of everydayness; we are free for God and thus also free from the burden of work and from the hustle and bustle of the world; free for shared festivals and celebrations, for human friendship and community. As God's day, the Sabbath is also the day of our humanity.

The rhythm of Sabbath is the humane and primeval rhythm of life established in creation. Religious festivals and celebrations are therefore the primeval cultural inheritance of human history. We may give up this primeval cultural inheritance only at the price of losing culture itself. We should rediscover this inheritance and fill it with new life. St. Irenaeus of Lyon (130–202 CE) put it this way: "The glory of God is the human being fully alive."

THE CHURCH YEAR AS "CHRIST YEAR"

Cultic festivals and the rhythm of Sabbath were the starting point for Jewish and Christian calendars of feast and festival days. The original motive leading to the exodus and liberation of the Israelites from bondage in Egypt was not the desire for political liberation, but the desire for the free exercise of religion. The negotiations of Moses and the elders with Pharaoh were centered on this question (see Exod 3:18, among other places). The Israelites departed from Egypt to achieve this freedom. Freedom of religion became the fundamental human right and was directly the basis of political freedom.

The Exodus began with the Passover meal (Exod 12:1–36). The word *Passover* means crossing over and passage, which occurred in the people of Israel's saving march through the Red Sea. Israel understood the success of this deliverance as the miraculous intervention of God. God delivered Israel into his own freedom (Exod 13—16). And so the annual celebration of Passover became the source and center of Jewish festivals and celebrations. This remembrance of the constitutive historical miracle of God, sealed in God's covenant with his people at Sinai, arose out of a primeval spring festival marking the renewal of cosmic order (Exod 19:4–6; 20:2).

This annual commemoration of the origins and founding of Israel also became a painful experience as the people often found themselves in new subjections and enslavements, in the Assyrian and Babylonian exiles and then again in the Hellenistic and Roman domination inside their own country. Even worse was acknowledging that the people of the covenant were again and again unfaithful, running after foreign gods. And so, this remembrance of a past miracle became the prophecy of a new exodus, a new liberation, and a new covenant (Isa 43:16–21; Ezek 20:33–44).

Jesus prophesied this new Passover at the Last Supper, which he celebrated with his disciples as a paschal or festival meal in connection with the Jewish Feast of Passover (Luke 22:15–19 and ff.; John 19:14). It became reality in his passover through death to resurrection. Jesus was thus the new paschal lamb offered for us (1 Cor 5:7; 1 Pet 1:19). Through his death and resurrection, he brought us deliverance from our deepest enslavement, the enslavement to sin and death. For through his resurrection, Jesus's death became the death of death, the final defeat of the power of death and the final victory of life (1 Cor 15:54–57). Through his death and resurrection, we who have been baptized into his death (Rom 6:3–11) have been set free for freedom (Gal 5:1) and have become a new creation (2 Cor 5:17 and Gal 6:15).

Already in the age of the apostles, the reality of this new creation led to the transference of the Sabbath from the seventh day to the first day of the week, the day of Jesus's resurrection and of the new creation, and to its celebration as the Lord's Day (Acts 20:7 and Rev 1:10). Thus, Sunday became the first feast day, what Vatican II calls "the foundation and kernel of the entire liturgical year" (Constitution on the Sacred Liturgy 106).[3] The Sabbath, which had become narrow and burdensome, was given back its original meaning in a deepened form. Jesus reminded believers that the Sabbath was made for humankind and not humankind for the Sabbath (Mark 2:27). As the day of the resurrection, the Christian Sabbath is a celebration of the new creation and of the freedom of the children of God for which the entire creation waits and watches with eager longing (Rom 8:19–30).

This weekly Passover led to the yearly Passover, the Easter celebration as Christianity's Passover celebration. It takes up the motif of the pagan festival of spring and changes it to a celebration of renewal and flourishing. It is the feast of Christian freedom and new life in which all partake through the Holy Spirit poured out at Pentecost, the fiftieth day after Easter, on young and old, women and men, slave and free from all parts of the then-known world (Acts 2:1–21). So, Easter and Pentecost are the feast of the birth of the church and of the church year that unites people of every race and culture, every state and stage of life, and unites them as the one people of God. The fact that the Latin church of the West and the Eastern churches do not celebrate Easter on the same day is thus a hard and painful wound within Christianity (see the appendix of the Constitution on the Sacred Liturgy).

As Judaism established its calendar of festival days, so the Christian church founded its liturgical year as a new annual and weekly rhythm fundamentally grounded in the celebration of Easter. The celebration of Easter begins with forty days of penitence and fasting (Lent); it has its center in the three days of the Sacred Triduum; and it lasts through the Feasts of Ascension and of the sending of the Spirit at Pentecost. The celebration of Easter is the middle and high point of the church year. In it we no longer celebrate a cosmic cycle of nature, but the new creation and new life anchored in historical acts of salvation. Easter continues to be celebrated throughout the entire year on every Sunday, each one a little Easter. In the celebration of the Eucharist, the whole church year is a celebration of the paschal mystery (Constitution on the Sacred Liturgy 5, 102–11). We sing or say the following in every eucharistic celebration: "We proclaim your death, O Lord, and profess your resurrection until you come again."

Again in a way similar to what happens in the Jewish Passover celebration, in the Christian paschal mystery there is also the remembrance of a past act of salvation as the hopeful forerunner of eschatological fulfillment and as the anticipatory celebration of the definitive, universal revelation of the coming (Parousia) of Christ, the definitive revelation of the new creation (2 Cor 5:17; Gal 6:15) and of the new heaven and the new earth (2 Pet 3:13; Rev 21:1), in which God will be all in all (1 Cor 15:28). And so, the liturgical year closes with the gospel story of the end of the world and, in the postconciliar liturgical reform, with the Feast of Christ the King as the celebration of the definitive revelation of Christ's all-encompassing reign, where all things are gathered and held together, where all find reconciliation and peace (Eph 1:10; Col 1:16–20 and ff.).

The Church Year

The saints' days, which we celebrate in the course of the liturgical year, belong within this larger context. From very early on, the memory of martyrs was commemorated liturgically. By their death in following Christ and in conformity to his death and resurrection, the paschal mystery has already been fulfilled in them. The confessors have already been victorious in this life in the spiritual battle with the evil one. Already in their earthly lives, they made space for new life; so, they gained the crown of life. Through the memory of the martyrs and of the holy women and men, we are reminded that the whole history of the church, even of the contemporary church, is a history of martyrs and holy ones and thus an ongoing paschal event.

Throughout the liturgical year, all Christians, having been baptized into the death of Jesus and thus born to the hope of new life (Rom 6:3–11), join together with the full Communion of Saints through and in Christ to walk this paschal way. This way leads through everyday sufferings and ultimately through death to new life and the Easter light of life. In this sense, on November 1, we celebrate the Feast of All Saints and, on the next day, we remember the souls of all the dead who have gone before us on the way to eternity. Our whole life is a passage from death to new life. As Augustine put it: "In the passion and resurrection of Christ the Lord, our own passage from life to death is sanctified."

Later, thematic feast days were added to the already established feasts of Christ and the saints. Particularly noteworthy are Trinity Sunday and the Feast of Corpus Christi. As meaningful as these feasts were and are, in their multiplication they were in danger of overloading the liturgical year; and the numerous thematic feasts and saints' days were in danger of obscuring its purpose of celebrating the mysteries of Christ (Constitution on the Sacred Liturgy 102ff.). The Second Vatican Council sought to emphasize more clearly the original meaning of the liturgical year as Christ's year and the Lord's year. In doing so it sought to make clearer that, throughout the entire church year, every aspect of our life is a pilgrimage with Christ on the way to eternal life.

The church year is a paschal year in two senses. It is so first through *anamnesis*, that is, through the remembering that makes past acts of salvation present now; and second, through anticipation, that is, through the anticipatory presence of the eschatological future begun once and for all times by Jesus Christ. Both senses are of the greatest importance.

Our present age is marked by a widespread historical amnesia. We are immersed in the cares and immediate concerns of the present. But whoever does not know where he has come from also does not know where he is now or where he should go next. Recalling the death and resurrection of Jesus and the memories of the martyrs and saints reminds us that, in the midst of all our losses, sufferings, worries, and finally even our dying, we are moving toward the victory of life and freedom. At the end of the second century, Tertullian (160–220 CE) wrote in his most famous work that "the blood of martyrs is the seed of the church" (Tertullian, *The Apology*, chap. 50). In times of crisis these words can give us confidence and hope for the future of the church. The church lives amid both the persecutions of the world and the consolations of God (St. Augustine, as cited by Vatican II's Dogmatic Constitution on the Church 8).

As Christians, however, we are not one-sidedly fixated on the past and imprisoned by it. Easter signifies victory over the burdens of the past as well as the primacy of the future over the past. Easter makes possible our openness to the greater future of God, our hope for new things, and our ability and courage—even in the face of disappointments and defeats—to begin anew again and again. Such hope gives us strength to remain courageous in the midst of difficulties and, if need be, bravely to face up to and risk the possibility of wounds and setbacks in the Christian struggle with the powers of falsehood and evil. At the same time, hope brings with it an Easter joy that already shines in this life and that we will experience in its fullness in blessed communion with God, toward which the church travels along the paschal way.

THE CHURCH YEAR AS TIME OF GRACE

A new reality dawned, fundamentally and once for all time, with the coming of Jesus Christ into the world. Jesus both announced and brought the fullness of time (Mark 1:14). The incarnation of the eternal Word, in whom and through whom everything was created and in whom all have light and life (John 1:2ff.; 14), means world history no longer amounts to the passing of time into nothingness. Time itself is fulfilled through the coming of God into time. The fullness of time has dawned in Christ (Gal 4:4; Eph 1:10). Christ came, in fact, so that we might have fullness of life (John 10:10). Out of *chronos*, time as fleeting and always unfulfilled, comes *kairos*, time fulfilled or graced time.[4] The Bible portrays this fullness of time through the image of a wedding and the joy surrounding it (Mark 2:19; Matt 22:1–14; 25:1–13; Rev 19:7, 9).

The arrival of this nuptial time of joy is celebrated in the Feasts of Christmas and the Epiphany of the Lord. The angel's message of joy and peace on earth is the message of Christmas (Luke 2:14). That era's expectation of the arrival of a peaceable kingdom under Caesar Augustus was thus fulfilled in a completely unexpected manner. And so, after Constantine's conversion, the Feast of Christmas could be celebrated on December 25, the day on which the Romans marked the birth of the unconquered sun god (*sol invictus*).[5] But the political expectation was fulfilled in a highly paradoxical way.

The message of joy and peace announced the birth of a weak child in the stable surrounded by shepherds, who were poor and despised in Jesus's day. Already in the *Magnificat* (Luke 1:46–55) and, again, in the Beatitudes of the Sermon on the Mount (Matt 5:3–12; Luke 6:20–26), the gospel gives special value to the poor, the little, the oppressed. This has nothing to do with a sentimental Christmas romanticism; rather, here the cross is casting its shadow in advance and helping us understand the incarnation as an emptying (Phil 2:5–8): for our sakes, the one who was rich became poor so that we might become rich (2 Cor 8:9).

The Feast of the Epiphany (January 6), celebrated as Christmas in Eastern Christianity, takes up the mystery cults of Rome and the East and changes their meaning: it celebrates the coming of the Lord as the light shining in the darkness of the world (Isa 9:1–6; 60:1–6); it celebrates the appearance of the star guiding the three wise men, representatives of the Gentiles, and leading them to Christ (Matt 2:1–12), in whom are hidden all the treasures of wisdom (Col 2:3). This feast day brings to the fore the universal character of the message about Jesus Christ. The Feast of the Baptism of the Lord publicly proclaims Jesus and marks the sanctification of the entire created order through Jesus's descent into the waters of the Jordan (Mark 1:9 and parallels).

Thus, from the fourth century onward, the Christmas season was added to the season of Easter. It begins with the First Sunday of Advent and lasts through the Feast of the Presentation of the Lord on February 2. Since Mary became God's entry gate into the world through her yes (Feast of the Annunciation of the Lord, March 25), there are important Marian feasts in the Christmas season: the Feast of the Immaculate Conception of Mary (December 8), the Feast of Mary the Mother of God (January 1), and the Feast of the Purification of Mary, the popular name for the Feast of the

Presentation of the Lord. While in the Western church the liturgical year begins on the First Sunday of Advent with preparation for the coming of the Lord, in the Eastern church it begins on September 1—with preparation for the Feast of the Birth of Mary (September 8). For the dawn of the new era began with the birth of Mary, Mother of God. Through her Assumption into heavenly glory (celebrated on August 15), Mary illuminates the path of the people of God on their pilgrim way.

All reality is sanctified in the coming of God into the world: all times become graced and holy times, and every moment becomes a moment of grace. "Now is the acceptable time...now is the day of salvation" (2 Cor 6:2). For Christians, time and history are not endless and boring, but are the limited time of here and now, always the time of expectation and decision. Thus, it is fitting to honor not only Sundays but also weekdays in order to sanctify everyday life in this world and in so doing to sanctify also ourselves. It is right, then, to make the most of this time (Eph 5:16). This is not meant in the sense of grabbing every chance for profitable economic activity, but as seeing time as our chance to prove ourselves through selfless acts of love. For love is the only thing that lasts; and, as love lasts, so will the works of love last (1 Cor 13:8, 13). Only these matter at the time of the world's judgment (Matt 25:31–46); they alone enter the lasting ledger of reality.

And so, liturgy must become *diakonia* (service). Jesus's word is definitive: "I desire mercy, not sacrifice" (Matt 9:13; 12:7). And so, in Germany, the season of Advent is marked by our *Adveniat* collections and with sales to support the missions.[6] Christmas often includes gifts and food for the poor. And Epiphany is connected with the actions of the *Sternsinger*.[7] In the seasons of Lent and Easter we take up collections for *Misereor*, we offer money from our Lenten fasting, and we contribute to *Bread for the World*.[8] And Pentecost is associated with collections for *Renovabis*.[9] All of these are new ways of making the liturgical year meaningful in our own time. They are intended to show that liturgy and the missionary renewal of the world belong together and form a single whole.

LOOKING AHEAD

As a time of grace, the church year is time given to us. We ourselves do not make it happen; it is a gift given to us as a binding directive. For grace always also brings a task with it. So the church year and its liturgy are neither museum pieces nor a surrealistic experiment. The seasons of the church year are not handed over to us to change as we wish, but like the church itself, the church year is always in need of renewal (Dogmatic Constitution on the Church 8).[10]

Throughout its history, the church year has adopted and transformed the heritage of many cultures: Eastern, Jewish, Hellenistic-Roman, Germanic. The church year has come to us in a historically particular form, affected by crises that its European heritage has undergone. So, again in our time, it may take new concrete forms as it engages with today's civilization and the cultures of other peoples. Thanks to the liturgical renewal movement of the twentieth century, especially since the Second Vatican Council, we have already taken many steps in this direction.

A major challenge remains in the twenty-first century: having left behind historicism and modernism,[11] we must now go further resolutely on the path outlined above in order to give our age and our lives new direction and meaning, new social cohesion and happiness; we must give human life new freedom and dignity. We are in the early stages of a new beginning. So, our task of renewal will doubtless keep us on our toes for a long while. Pope John Paul II prophetically predicted that the renewal of Sundays and feast days as times of grace for human beings will be decisive for the identity of the church in the third millennium.[12]

CHAPTER TWO

"THE WORD BECAME FLESH" (REFLECTIONS FOR ADVENT AND CHRISTMAS)

"YOU KNOW WHAT TIME IT IS" (FIRST SUNDAY OF ADVENT, YEAR A: ROMANS 13:11–14)

Like few other times, the season of Advent asks us who we are and where we stand. The noisy and busy world around us becomes all the more hectic during precisely these days. In a completely uninhibited way, that world is characterized by possessing and the desire to possess, by market and consumption. "You know what time it is" (Rom 13:11). In our present situation we must allow this word of the Apostle to strike us in a powerful way. Is it really the most important things that so capture our attention? Indeed, isn't it time for us to wake from our sleep?

Jesus Christ is the light, the way, the truth, and the life; he is Lord of the new era—our era. "Christian, remember your dignity," as Pope St. Leo the Great put it, "and be aware that you share in God's own nature. Do not return to your former baseness by a life unworthy of that dignity."[1] Let us take Advent as a chance to remember again our dignity as baptized persons.

Awareness of what time it is and of who we are before God brings consequences with it. The Apostle Paul tells us the first of those consequences: whatever needs the cover of darkness is to be set aside. To name the sore spots, the features of a world that is without foundation and passing away, Paul takes examples from the social decay of Rome in his day: reveling and drunkenness, debauchery and licentiousness, quarrelling and jealousy (Rom 13:13). All of these undermine our human dignity. They are signs and symptoms of a broken world that is passing away. Surely, we do not have to look very hard to see that we ourselves are implicated here!

And this is only the first step. Paul takes another: along with laying aside the works of darkness comes putting on the armor of light (Rom 13:12). The change in images is not insignificant. "Armor of light" is a harsher, more militant image than if Paul had written of the "works of light." We Christians are to be active, even militant in taking up the armor of light.

Such militant language and attitudes have become quite foreign to us Christians today. We prize tolerance above all. In fact, can we even name a time when we have put on the armor of light? Unfortunately, have we not more frequently taken up the armor and the weapons of this world? But we Christians have every reason to lay them aside. It is not by means of force that we are to fight and win the day, but with the word of truth, the breastplate of righteousness, the shield of faith, the sword of the Spirit, and not least by our unceasing prayer (see Eph 6:14–18). In this spiritual sense, we should still be the church militant.

Paul adds a third statement to his twin calls for setting aside the works of darkness and taking up the armor of light.

He intensifies what he has already said and calls us to "put on the Lord Jesus Christ" as a new garment (Rom 13:14). Here he says the decisive thing, the thing on which all else depends. We are told to put aside the old Adam, the one of darkness, of illusions, and of lies, and put on the reality of Christ. In baptism, you have been brought to this new reality. Jesus Christ is the true reality. He is the image of God. We are restored to God's image in him. Our true humanity and the ground and purpose of our existence are revealed in him. He is our hope. In him we move into the dawn of the new day, of the new era.

"Do Not Quench the Spirit" (Third Sunday of Advent, Year B: 1 Thessalonians 5:16–24)

The Apostle calls out to his community and admonishes them urgently: "Do not quench the Spirit" (1 Thess 5:19).

It is obviously quite possible for us human beings to block, suppress, and make ineffective the mighty Spirit of God. Let us not quench this Spirit, nor dry it up within ourselves; let us take care that the Spirit does not get lost or become slowly extinguished within us. The real danger in our time does not come from those who oppose the church, but from our own indifference and apathy. Our self-satisfaction and inertia are the death of faith.

Today, in an age when everything is planned, counted, measured, and weighed, it is difficult to recognize the significance of the Spirit. We live in a time when material things are most often given priority. They hang on us like leaden weights and drag us down. We must freely open our eyes and ears in order to have a feel for what the Spirit is doing in this time of ours; we must have an open and ready heart, faithfully making space for the delicate plant that has been planted within us to grow—and thus not quenching the Spirit.

One sign of the living Spirit in the contemporary church consists in church membership now primarily being a matter of free choice and in the likelihood of its being even more so in the future. In the past, so it is often said, "people" only went to the church because everyone else went, and not going meant excluding oneself from or being excluded by one's neighbors. Today, and again even more in the future, it is *I* who goes to church because I am convinced of the importance of faith and of how beneficial it is to my life. The church of the future will be ever more a church made up of people who have made their own responsible decision for membership. Perhaps that will mean fewer members than in the past. It does not say anywhere in the Gospels that one day all human beings will be Christians. And, if those who are Christian are so out of inner conviction, then that is essentially a sign of progress. For, according to the Second Vatican Council's Pastoral Constitution on the Church in the Modern World, conscience is "the most secret core and sanctuary of [the human person]" (no. 16). In conscience, we can hear the voice of God; God's Spirit is at work in us through our conscience.

It is a matter of making space within ourselves, within our own conscience, for the Holy Spirit—and then of responding to that Spirit in personal prayer. Unless we do so, we will not be able to live a human existence, let alone a Christian existence, in this fast-paced time of ours. Let us not quench this Spirit!

This saying from Paul is both intended and able to give us courage to surrender to the dynamism of the Spirit and so to gain a new future. It says to us, the warmth of the Spirit is still there under the ashes; let it be rekindled into a blazing fire!

LIGHT IN THE DARKNESS (CHRISTMAS, MASS AT MIDNIGHT: LUKE 2:1–14)

Our cries and longing for salvation, for peace, for healing have not been in vain. Our cry has not died away unheard. We need not give in to skepticism and resignation. We need not collapse in hopelessness. A light has brightened the darkness. God has given us the peace that the world cannot give. God has not remained remote from us. With infinite mercy, God emptied himself and condescended to share our life. The eternal Word of God became flesh, one of us. God has taken the dark streets and dangerous alleys with us, beginning from a search for shelter in Bethlehem, from the simple stable all the way to unjust conviction, to suffering and death on the cross.

God has made our cause God's own cause, and so has made his eternal divine life our salvation. God became a human being, as the church fathers put it, so that we might share God's eternal life. Therein lies our true human dignity! Christian faith breaks open the vicious circle into which we have fallen; it is light in the darkness and strength for living. In the end, faith promises us eternal life. Conversely, the eclipse of God is also the eclipse of humanity. It leaves us alone and hopeless. But contemplation of the miracle of Christmas can open us anew to the value and dignity of each and every human being. The incarnation of God is the foundation of a new humanism, a Christian humanism.

Whoever believes in the miracle of that holy night may live from grace. She may be sure of this. In allying himself with us human beings, with each one of us, God speaks an irrevocable yes to each of us. God says, "Yes, I want you to be.[2] I will not let you fall. I will love you for all eternity." If we live from this grace, our life is not simply the sum of our accomplishments and merits; it is also not permanently mired in our guilt and errors. However great our errors are, God's grace is always greater; we need only be willing to turn back to God. God's gracious mercy reigns above and beyond everything that exists. In the child lying in the manger, God's mercy has shone on us for all time.

In this child, the goodness and kindness of God has appeared. Goodness and kindness are thus the meaning of the world, the meaning and task of our lives.

In this child, then, the truth of our lives has also appeared. Jesus Christ himself is the way, the truth, and the life. Whoever follows Christ no longer needs to run after false illusions and live his own lies.

Such a person does not make her own selfishness the measure of all things and does not confuse freedom with self-will. She knows the measure that God has set for us and the path that is pointed out to us in Jesus Christ. In this child in the manger God has definitively shown us wherein our true humanity lies: in living from God's love and in living in a way that shares this love. To act in this truth and live in this love is to live in the light.

PEACE ON EARTH (CHRISTMAS, MASS AT MIDNIGHT: LUKE 2:1–14)

"Glory to God in the highest heaven, and on earth peace among those whom he favors!" (Luke 2:14). In this message of the great heavenly host, the whole radiance, joy, and festive rejoicing of the Holy Night come together as the focal point of a spotlight. The great promise is heard from out of the night sky, above the fields where the simple and anonymous shepherds keep watch over their animals. Individuals and whole peoples had long been waiting for it. The new message of God now goes out into the midst of everyday life and work, of human limitation, of ordinary and even boring life. Now God fulfills his promise of salvation, now God glorifies his name in the birth of his Son, and so God's praise is sung: "Glory to God in the highest heaven, and on earth peace among those whom he favors."

Peace on earth: this promise of God meets a primal desire in all of us. It was not only then, in the past, that individuals and whole peoples had to live in darkness, even in the "land of...darkness" (Isa 9:2) under an oppressive yoke. All who live in darkness see a great light. The light shines on all those living in the land of darkness.

A stream of warmth flows into our history, a stream of grace. We sense this in all the hopes we have as human beings, in our yearning that what we see is not everything but calls out for a far greater fulfillment. In the depths of our hearts, we are all hoping for something more than the grayness of everyday life and of our daily routine, more than our consuming, which can never fill us. We all dream a dream of a different, better, more healed, and more peaceful world. About such a world we can acknowledge this: yes, it should be that way, it would be beautiful, true, and good. It is about this world that the angels' song of praise and promise speaks. Peace—on earth.

This goodness, this peace has appeared among us in Jesus of Nazareth, to save us through the mercy of God. In the person of Jesus Christ, God has not remained off by himself. God did not hold onto divine life for himself, but passed it on to others. God himself became human in his Son, in order to share his peace and divine life with the world. In Jesus Christ, the whole fullness of God has appeared as a gift given to all and including all. In him the abundant wisdom and eternal mystery of God has been revealed. He embraces and unites all that is in heaven and on the earth. In him the fullness of time has appeared.

The turning point of history has arrived in the child lying in the manger. Here is the key, the midpoint and the goal of all human history. The divine child is the decisive response to the longings of our lives. This child shows us who God is: self-giving love. And this child also shows us who we are: those loved by God, those whom God seeks out and brings home.

"Christ, the Savior, Is Born" (Christmas, Mass at Midnight: Luke 2:1–14)

The divine child in the manger, the simple shepherds in the field, the message and song of the angels: all these stir the deepest chords of our hearts, and a light comes forth from them into the darkness of our world. Immediately a thought comes to us: Yes, the miracle had to happen, the miracle of another, a better, a new world. For those who do not believe, for those who no longer believe or do not yet believe, Christmas is a longing and a hope that simply belongs to our humanity, a hope without which no one can live.

And so, what remains of the Christmas spirit? How is it possible for us to sing, as we do at the end of the last verse of *Silent Night*, that "Christ, the savior, is born"? What does the message of the angel in the Christmas gospel mean: "To you is born this day in the city of David a Savior, who is the Messiah, the Lord" (Luke 2:11)? Many ask, Is that really so? Does he really help the poor and oppressed; will he really comfort the lonely and the abandoned? Are we even convinced that we need a savior, a redeemer, a liberator? Is there any such thing as salvation, as redemption?

Precisely in this situation we should not suppress these Christmas longings; we do not need to feel ashamed of them. They show us that our longing for salvation and redemption belongs ineradicably to us. Without it we are unable to live a life that is truly human. But we must again become conscious of this truth: salvation and redemption do not spring up from us, from our own efforts. We are not able to escape the infernal cycle of evil by our own efforts. We cannot create the new world and we are not in control of our own destiny. We cannot save ourselves.

Expectations of salvation from within the world have been deceived. We must rethink our expectations and reorient our lives. A new beginning must be made; a fundamental turning-around is called for. The savior can only come from above; only God can redeem us.

This is the joyful message of Christmas: "Christ the savior is born." "To you is born this day in the city of David a Savior." The turning has happened, because God himself has turned toward us once and for all time. On the face of this child in the manger, God has once and for all time radiated the splendor of his glory and peace. So, we may sing, "Now rejoice, O Christians, sing in jubilation…Christ the Savior descended to us. Come, let us worship."[3]

Light shines above the manger. Light gives us direction and orientation; it opens new perspectives. The child in the manger is this light. He opens our eyes to see who God is and who we ourselves are. He shows us the God who is not somewhere off in the distance, unreachable through our prayers and lamentations, but the God who sees our distress and hears our cry, the God who himself becomes human, to be with us wholly and in everything, the God of kindness, love, and mercy. Thus, the child in the manger teaches us to see our lives in a new light, in the light of an eternal love that accepts and affirms every single one of us. We are not alone and abandoned, our world is no longer dark, cold, and empty. A light shines on us in the night, a light for our way, a light that gives us courage and hope.

"Christ the savior is born." He is our savior from darkness and hopelessness, our savior from selfishness and death. He is the savior who gives eternal validity to our longing and hope, who fulfills them in a manner surpassing all expectation. Come, let us worship!

"I Love You, You, the World, and Humankind" (Christmas, Mass at Midnight: Luke 2:1–14)

For us Christians, Christmas is more than a passing mood and vague longing. The mood of Christmas that enthralls us is only a distant reminder of what is much deeper in us human beings, yes, of what we human beings are. We are certainly embodied beings, moved by many moods, feelings, and expectations. Most deeply, however, we are beings touched by an unfathomable mystery. We are always underway, questioning, seeking, and hoping. We may have and possess many things, but as humans we are always more than what we have and possess.

In the first pages of the Bible, we are told that we have been created according to the image and likeness of God. And so only the infinite God is big enough to fill the whole breadth and depth and enormity of our human heart. "Our heart is restless until it rests in you, God," wrote one of the deepest thinkers of Christian history.[4] We could also say the following: We are poor people who, in a thousand conscious or unconscious ways, look and hope for what the message of Christmas proclaims: that God himself has come into our weak and unfulfilled humanity to fill it with his fullness, light, and life.

This is what Christmas tells us: there is one who hears me, one who knows me, one who is like me with my strengths and my limitations, my cares and my questions. There is someone who holds on to me, even when my powers dwindle and I fail. There is someone who accepts me, who says yes to me. God really is with us; God is among us. In Jesus Christ,

God has accepted every human being decisively and with infinite love, has united himself to every one of us.

The child in the manger is the decisive and concrete response to the questions and longing of our lives. This child shows us who God is: self-giving love; this child also shows us who we are: those infinitely loved by God.

At Christmas, the one who was rich comes into our history in poverty, so that by his poverty we might become rich (see 2 Cor 8:9). The one who is the light goes into the darkness and the abyss, so that the world might become brighter in him. As the church father St. Ambrose put it, "He descended…into our footsteps so that he might call us back to life by following in his footsteps."[5] He took up our path so that he might lead us to his path. He walked our way in order to direct it back toward God. He has gone all our ways, the happy ones, the overwhelmed and bitter ones, the fast ways of youth and the slowed-down ways of the elderly. He has taken all things on himself in order to rescue all.

In the incarnation of his Son, God has spoken the word of truth in love. Karl Rahner has described it in this way: "God has spoken into the world his last, his deepest, his most beautiful word…a word that can no longer be revoked because it is God's definitive deed, because it is God himself in the world. And this word means: I love you, you, the world and humankind."[6]

WHY DID GOD BECOME HUMAN? (CHRISTMAS, MASS DURING THE DAY: JOHN 1:1–18)

"The Word became flesh" (John 1:14). God became a human being: that is the message of Christmas. In the eleventh century, a monk by the name of Anselm (1033–1109 CE), living first in French Normandy and later in Canterbury in England, asked, "Why did God become a human being?" He wrote a famous book whose title is that very question: *Cur Deus Homo?* Why did God become human? His response—summarized in a brief formula—was this: Sin is so great, so powerful in the world, that only God could remedy it; only God is great and powerful enough to bring us healing and redemption. This is the same response that the Apostle Paul had given in the Letter to the Romans: "Where sin increased, grace abounded all the more" (Rom 5:20).

Grace has been bestowed upon us. Christmas is the antidote to resignation and hopelessness. Christmas says to us, the good star of Bethlehem also shines on us. God has committed himself to us. God has not let us down. God himself has come, has become human for our sake and for our salvation. And so the angel says to the shepherds in the fields of Bethlehem, "Do not be afraid!" (Luke 2:10). Do not be anxious, take courage! For joy, confidence, and hope have been announced to us.

"The Word became flesh." God became a human being. This tells us something, indeed something decisive about who God is. He is a God of human beings, a God who is concerned about us. Someone even put it this way: God is downright crazy about us human beings. God is in love with us. As the Christmas gospel puts it, God showers us with "grace upon grace" (John 1:16).

For the God who reveals himself to us at Christmas is no nameless God, but a personal God who has a heart for human beings, whose heart has mercy on us, whose heart is turned inside out in response to our human suffering. In Jesus Christ this God runs after us, seeks us out, himself becoming human to experience in his own body all the distress, all the pain and suffering, violence, abandonment and loneliness, all the helplessness of a small child, the loss of home and country of young parents, and later the disloyalty of friends and the hatred of opponents. In all of this, God became like us in order to be close to us in everything.

God has bound himself to us once for all time. Thus, God is fully divine precisely in becoming fully human and revealing himself as a God in love with human beings.

This is a completely unimaginable message: the eternal, infinite, incomprehensible, invisible God became a finite human being, became tangible and visible in the flesh. In the face of this mystery of incomprehensible, eternal love radically emptying itself, we can only kneel in wonder and adoration. We must learn this posture anew in our own day.

What is a human being? In the incarnation of his Son, God has given a clear and final response to this question about human identity. The response rings out: the human being, every human being, is a being in need of mercy and even more of love. We need mercy because, of our own strength, we are unable to free ourselves from our distress and the misery in which we often find ourselves. We rely on God's mercy and on merciful human beings.

Our greatness is that for God, we—every single one of us—are creatures deserving of love. We so deserve love that God himself fell in love with us and became a human being in order to be close to us. Therefore, every human being is of infinite value, whether native or foreigner, healthy or ill, old or disabled, rich or poor. For God and in God's sight, every human being is worthy of love and of life. God wanted to become a human being, so that we could share in God's own divine life.

God has opened a new history of true humanity, overcoming our selfish, vain, arrogant, violent nature. At Christmas God became small and poor; God "emptied himself, taking the form of a slave" (see Phil 2:7). God is in solidarity with us; he shares our life! God shares our weak humanity, in order also to share with us God's own divine life.

And so, why did God become a human being? God wanted to show both who he is and who we are. God did not only want to show it, but to model and live it bodily. God wanted to bring the warmth of divine love into our world turned tired and cold, into our frozen world. God wanted to break the ice between himself and us, and between us and our fellow human beings. Where sin increased, there grace abounded all the more. "Grace upon grace" (John 1:16) is the last word. Christmas is the triumph of grace.

"A Rose Has Sprung Up" (Christmas, Mass during the Day)

"A rose has sprung up, from a tender root."[7] At Christmas the ancient promise has come true in a wonderful way. Every small rose that blooms from a thorny shrub, and certainly every child born is a miracle. Yet, in a particular way, this child in the manger is the miracle of the unexpected new beginning that only God can bring. He is the delicate little rose, which—like the first flowers of spring after a harsh winter—shows that life continues, that we need not despair, that hope is possible. This child in the manger says to us, God is here, right in our midst. God has not forgotten or abandoned us; God has come and forever remains with us and for us. We are not alone, not a single one of us. God has spoken God's irrevocable yes to humankind, to each individual human being. We may risk living our lives since God has done the same. We pray in the liturgy of Christmas:

"O God, you wonderfully created human nature." Yes, truly, each human being, with all her strengths and abilities, is a miracle: every human being comes from God with a very unique dignity that no one may take away! "And even more wonderfully restored its dignity"

(from the Opening Prayer for Christmas Mass during the Day).[8] *Despite all the wounds and deformations that we human beings have caused ourselves by sin, you, God, have given us an even greater dignity. For, by becoming human yourself and definitively binding yourself to us, you have given us human beings in all our frailty and brokenness a new splendor, a new status, and a new dignity; and you have made all of us your children, your sons and daughters.*

In the midst of his parents' lack of home and of homeland, in the midst of the poverty of the simple shepherds in the field, the warm splendor of the light of God's love and mercy shines on the face of the child in the manger and out into this cold world. Since then, the world and our lives are much more than a series of chance events; naked self-interest and brute force do not rule the day. A miracle has occurred; something completely unexpected and beyond any human capacity to make happen has taken place. In this child in the manger, awe-filled, we may now see the glory of God and be filled with grace and truth. This is the warm light of Christmas. It is a sign, a symbol showing us that the dark night of our life and our world has become a silent, holy night.

Above all else, let us accept the light of Christmas into our hearts. This light is not like a glaring floodlight. At Christmas, God comes into the world in poverty and simplicity. God comes into the everydayness of our lives. And God can make something of the broken pieces of our lives. We must simply learn again the stance of the shepherds of Bethlehem, the stance of reverence and worship before something that is greater than ourselves, before something that sustains our lives and embraces us with grace and favor, before something that can give us strength and courage, the posture of worship before God and the child in the manger, God's Son become human.

Among the happy "signs of the time" in our day is that, in the wake of the peace process in the Middle East, Bethlehem is no longer an occupied city.[9] Whoever has visited the Church of the Nativity there knows that one can enter only through a very low doorway; one must stoop down in order to enter. This seems symbolic of God making himself small as he came into this world. And so we must not puff ourselves up. We must humble ourselves if we want to approach the child in the manger, and we must bow down before our fellow human beings. We are greatest when we kneel down and pray.

Christmas gives us the answer to the question about the mystery of our lives. Christmas says to us that, despite everything and in everything, there is a great mystery that surrounds and sustains us human beings, a mystery that gives us dignity and value. That mystery took flesh in Jesus Christ. Let us remain true to this mystery. With the Prophet Isaiah, let us carry hope that, on the seemingly dead stump of our lives, of our world, of our church, a small rose will indeed bloom, a rose of new life, new hope, new enthusiasm in faith.[10] Let us live this hope.

"A rose has sprung up." And, as the song continues, "With its clear light, it dispels the darkness...helps us in all trouble, and saves us from sin and death."[11]

DOING THE TRUTH IN LOVE—HEARING AND LIVING THE WORD OF GOD (REFLECTIONS FOR ORDINARY TIME)

INTRODUCTION: DOING THE TRUTH IN LOVE[1]

The gospel message is as relevant today as ever. Precisely for us today it is the one necessary thing. In recent years, we have restored the buildings of traditional towns and villages; most of our old churches have also been renovated at quite an expense. But have we also renewed the spirit from which our churches and cultural monuments have arisen? That spirit was the spirit of Christian faith. Today, on account of our wealth, are we not in danger of losing the soul of our culture and our own souls as well? Our situation is like that of the people in front of the Tower of Babel: nothing seems unattainable, everything seems possible (Gen 11:6). But for what purpose? Are we moving in the right direction? Do we even have a direction?

If we want not only to survive but also to live truly human lives, then we need not only clean air and green trees, however necessary these are. Our souls also want to breathe healthily. We can live humanly only if we do the truth in love.

Truth does not only mean saying true things. Truth means openness to true reality, on which one can build and in which one can trust in life as well as in death. The truth of our life is God's unshakeable loyalty, God's unreserved yes to each of us and to all of us together as the people of God. God spoke this yes once and for all times in Jesus Christ. Jesus is the "way, and the truth, and the life" (John 14:6). He is the key, center, and goal of all human history, the Alpha and Omega (Rev 1:8). He is the salvation of the world, he alone. He, Jesus Christ, should then be both our way and leader in faith (Heb 12:2).

The gospel without additions, but also without compromises is the most important asset that we can bring into the future. For the truth frees us (John 8:32) from quickly changing moods and fashions. Truth gives our life foundation and content. It is the ground of our hope.

One may ask, How can we do this? An answer rings forth from the Apostle Paul: Do "the truth in love" (Eph 4:15). The truth of Jesus Christ wants to be put into action (John 3:21). God's Word has become flesh and wants to be "situated" in a consistent and concrete way, enfleshed in our world: in our families, our workplaces, and our free time. Jesus Christ meets us concretely in the sick and disabled, the poor and the suffering. And he is effectively present in the church. It is his body and is to be built up in love (Eph 4:16). It is the house of truth, a sign of God in the world.

What would have become of the gospel without the church, which has preserved, collected, and handed down the biblical writings until the present day? Is the church not also our true mother in faith? Where does Jesus Christ encounter us more intensively than in the celebration of the Eucharist?

Indeed, whoever does not say yes to the church has also not fully said yes to Jesus Christ, its head and Lord. As the great theologian and bishop Augustine put it: it is a matter of the whole Christ, of Jesus Christ as the head and of Jesus Christ in his members. We are all this church.

To Bring Good News to the Poor (Third Sunday in Ordinary Time, Year C: Luke 1:1–4; 4:14–21)

Anointed and sent, "to bring good news to the poor" (Luke 4:18). In Latin, the second half of this text reads: *evangelizare pauperibus*. With these inaugural words of his preaching—of what we could call his first sermon in his hometown of Nazareth—Jesus summarizes the whole of his mission and work.

It is a message about the God who promises that the deserts will bloom—not just the deserts of sand and stone, but the deserts of our lives and our world with all their barrenness and dryness. It is a message about the God who gives life and desires life, the God who is the friend of life and who promises life in its fullness.

"Strengthen the weak hands, and make firm the feeble knees….'Be strong, do not fear! Here is your God'" (Isa 35:3–4). This God desires the salvation of the whole person. God wants the blind to see, the deaf to hear, the lame to walk freely, the imprisoned to be set free. A year of grace should be proclaimed: freedom from sin and guilt should be announced, with forgiveness and reconciliation and the infinite mercy of God.

Evangelizare pauperibus—"bringing good news to the poor." Wherever we read in the Old and New Testament, we come upon God's preferential option for the poor, for little ones, for people on the margins, children and women, the disenfranchised, the oppressed, the sick, and the dying.

Who are these poor today? They are the homeless, refugees throughout the world, human beings who live at or below the poverty line, the disabled, the violated and abused, young people who are never given a chance to make their way into a career and so are left behind by life. Certainly, there is such material poverty, but not only that. There is cultural, intellectual, and spiritual poverty and neglect; there is the loss of guidance, of support, of courage, and of orientation; there is the experience of meaninglessness and hopelessness. Not least of all there is also religious impoverishment, the now common experience of a spiritual desert and emptiness that robs people of the deepest meaning and sense of human fulfillment, and leaves them inwardly poor and mentally crippled and warped.

Evangelizare pauperibus—"bringing good news to the poor." To do this means to live in the shadow of the cross and become poor. It means to live simply, without making demands on the world's goods. It means not holding oneself above others, but sharing one's time and whole life as well as one's money. It means not making demands, but being able to let go and accept when things turn out differently from the way we thought or hoped they would, differently from what we had our minds set on. It also means accepting a lack of success, a lack of prestige. Spiritual poverty means creating space for and remaining open to God's Holy Spirit, who is always good for surprises and whose ways are not always the ways we have planned.

The Sermon on the Mount
(Fourth Sunday in Ordinary Time, Year A:
Matthew 5:1–12a)

In the Sermon on the Mount (Matt 5—7), the evangelist summarizes Jesus's entire agenda; in it, at the beginning of his Gospel, Matthew gives us a kind of summary of the whole gospel message.

When we read the Sermon on the Mount, do we become scared, wince, and ask in a subdued and uncomfortable way, Is it really that way? Am I able to do that? Is anyone able to do it? Is what is written there doable in this world? Or is it more like an unrealistic dream, pious perhaps but escapist?

Indeed, the contrast could hardly be greater between what is written here and what matters in our world, how people think, how they judge, how they behave, how they live, or more precisely, how we think, how we judge, how we behave, and how we live. For, where in our world are the poor, those who mourn, and the persecuted considered blessed? Don't we think of those who are healthy, wealthy, cheerful, successful as "blessed"?

But, let us read and hear precisely what is said here! It does not say, you shall, you must, you must not; one or another thing being commanded and something else being forbidden. The Sermon on the Mount is no catalog of dos and don'ts. Unfortunately, many people understand Christianity as just such a moralistic catalog of dos and don'ts. As such, it scares them off. It goes beyond our human strength. It overwhelms all of us immeasurably.

The Sermon on the Mount is the gospel; it is good and liberating news. It does not begin with a litany of dos and don'ts. It does not demand great moral achievements. It is not joyless moralism. On the contrary, it begins with beatitudes:

"Blessed are," so the text proclaims nine times. The Sermon on the Mount is a message of grace.

The God of Jesus is close to human beings, a God for human beings. God is merciful. God stoops down to those in the dust. God cares most of all for the poor, those who mourn, the merciful, the peacemakers, the ridiculed and persecuted. God cares for all who are marginalized, who are not seen under the radar, who are unnoticed in this world and do not count. God respects not only the successful and the winners; God also thinks of the defeated and oppressed. They are called blessed; they will be praised as divine. They are allowed to breathe. They are allowed to hope.

So, the Beatitudes of the Sermon on the Mount are a message of great hope. This message was initially directed to the people at that time. For the vast majority of them, the situation was humanly hopeless. They were extremely poor, harassed by the Roman occupying power, bled dry and exploited by their henchmen, and let down by their leaders. Jesus tells these people that the promises of the prophets are now true and real. Blessed are you! To you belongs the kingdom of heaven.

God himself vouches for the fact that, in the end, the world is not ruled by lies, violence, and injustice. God vindicates life; God brings the truth to light; God builds up justice and proves that love is victorious. Life and love are more powerful than death; they pass over into eternal life. In the end, God will be all in all forever.

This hope is not at all wishful thinking; it awakens people and spurs them on. Just as God does, so should we also embrace the poor, those who mourn, those who seek justice; and we should commit ourselves to them. "Be merciful, just as your Father is merciful," so says Jesus in another place (Luke 6:36). On this account are the merciful and the peacemakers called blessed.

The Sermon on the Mount is an encouragement. It gives us the courage and strength to realize God's desires in this world in exemplary ways. It demands justice for all, especially for the poor and the little ones. It does so because the rich and powerful can help themselves, and in general do help themselves. The poor are the materially poor. They are among us in mostly hidden ways.

It's like a person walking with a lantern in the middle of the pitch-dark night: the lantern lights the way for her, but it does so only to the extent that she herself keeps walking. In the same way, the gospel is a light that enlightens our minds and encourages our actions. The gospel does not decrease our responsibility; it calls that responsibility forth, leads it onward, encourages and strengthens it. We cannot bring forth the reign of God through our actions. But through works of justice and love, God already now brings forth his reign in exemplary and symbolic ways.

"BLESSED ARE..."
(FOURTH SUNDAY IN ORDINARY TIME, YEAR A: MATTHEW 5:1–12A)

The Beatitudes of the Sermon on the Mount are a bedrock of biblical teaching and a founding document of our faith life. In their powerful and memorable language, the Beatitudes are our vision of a new and different world as we daily and painfully experience our present world in its injustice and brutality, in its ruthlessness and blatant selfishness. They are a message of confidence and hope for all the oppressed and suffering, for all the millions who, humanly speaking, have nothing to expect in their lives. They are the expression of a deep longing that lives in all of us. They stand against all the resignation that so often creeps into our lives, given the current state of the world; they also stand against the sinister nihilism that gnaws at our hearts when we think that nothing makes sense anymore. They are words that we urgently need today.

Yet, aren't these words a boundless imposition on our lives, in which we are daily forced to fight for survival and pressed toward the assertiveness and drivenness without which life is impossible? Was German philosopher Friedrich Nietzsche (1844–1900) right when he saw in the Beatitudes a belittling and slandering of strong and vigorous persons, when he detected in them a scent of the resentment of the weak and deficient?[2]

Or, perhaps the Beatitudes are nothing more than a soft consolation that holds us back from resolutely taking the things of this world into our own hands and finally bringing justice, peace, and freedom.

All of these are temptations to which Christians have succumbed throughout history and still succumb to today. The Sermon on the Mount has not had an easy time with us, and we have to struggle with it. For, what is said in this bedrock element of Jesus's reign-of-God preaching is unprecedented and paradoxical. What does it mean that the poor are praised as happy, the hungry as filled? How can one defeat and eliminate unjust violence nonviolently?

The solution to our so disastrously deadlocked situation can only be salvation, a whole new start, a beginning that cannot come from our hopeless world, but from God alone. So, the vision of the Sermon on the Mount presupposes a fundamental reversal of all relationships. It is inseparable from God's promise that he, God alone, will bring forth a new heaven and a new earth and that then all tears will be wiped away, then death will be no more, then there will be neither mourning, nor crying out, nor hardship. For God, the Lord of history, is making all things new (see Rev 21:4–5).

For the evangelist Matthew, this vision of the coming reign of God and God's justice is no mere dream; for him, it has already become reality in the appearance and conduct of Jesus. He is the new beginning, the concrete form of the Beatitudes of the Sermon on the Mount. He is gentle and humble in heart (Matt 11:29), and his gentleness was contagious. In his presence people were healed and could breathe again.

The beatitude about the meek must become the regular way of life of the Christian community. For whoever relies entirely on God, as Jesus did, can be calm enough to bring gentleness, humility, friendliness, mildness, and forgiveness, in the face of all recklessness, quick-temperedness, and drivenness, pretentiousness, arrogance, and pride— and to trust that precisely and only these qualities of meekness heal the wounds, make peace, and internally free and redeem us. And, if the church adopts Jesus's beatitude of the poor, then it can and should carry out the option for the poor and stand with those who have no voice and no chance in this world.

The meek, so says the Sermon on the Mount, will inherit the earth; in the language of the scriptures this means they are to lead the world. The world is entrusted to them, into their responsibility. We Christians can perform this service of peace together. Together we must face the questions and challenges of our time. To our world that so often loses its orientation and perspective, we together must witness to the trust and hope of the Beatitudes, and we must say to all, yes, it makes sense to do good and to commit ourselves to justice and peacemaking.

The Sermon on the Mount is the only realistic alternative, and one upon which many more people than we commonly realize are waiting.

Infinite Mercy
(Fourth Sunday in Ordinary Time, Year A:
Matthew 5:1–12a)

Jesus proclaims the merciful God who does not impose on the sinner his just and deserved punishment, but forgives and pardons the one who repents. Jesus himself is the Good Shepherd who pursues the lost sheep and brings it back—even giving his life for us sinners. The heart of God opens up to us in mercy, for God himself is love.

Here we encounter the heart of our faith. The Christian faith is not primarily about what we do and accomplish, or about what we are not supposed or allowed to do, but about what God is doing for us. It is not first of all about our right action, but about God making us right, forgiving and pardoning us, despite our lack of right action—and all that so that we then do likewise, removing others' burdens and supporting them, giving them a chance for a new start, forgiving and pardoning and so beginning again together.

This is more than justice; it is mercy and love. It is not that mercy replaces justice and leaves it without force. It does not undercut justice, but outbids it. It is the greater and true justice. For I am only truly just to another person when I accept her completely, loving her and saying to her, I want you to be.

Each of us gets lost in his life again and again; each of us gets lost in superficialities and trifles, in guilt and sin. If any of us were to claim we have nothing to reproach ourselves for, we would in fact be in error and lost in self-deception. We all rely on forgiveness; we all need salvation. All of us rely on the infinite mercy of God; all of us need daily repentance. The call to be merciful to our fellow human beings is repeated again and again in the Gospels. We need only think

41

of the Beatitudes of the Sermon on the Mount: "Blessed are the merciful, for they will receive mercy" (Matt 5:7). Jesus even makes our mercy toward the poor, the persecuted, and those suffering in any way the criterion of his last judgment (see Matt 25:40). Mercy is the measure by which we will all finally be measured. In the end, we can bring nothing with us; everything that we have done in love and mercy will endure. Love alone finally matters.

WITNESS TO HOPE
(FOURTH SUNDAY IN ORDINARY TIME, YEAR A: MATTHEW 5:1–12A)

The Beatitudes of the Sermon on the Mount are, for Jesus, the bedrock. They belong to the very heart of Jesus's teaching. With the ninefold "blessed are" sayings, Jesus places everything that has happened in the past, is happening now, and will happen in the future under the great promise of God. He does not align himself with the doomsayers who see failure, doom, and disaster everywhere. He begins his preaching, not with the words "Woe to you," but rather with the words "Blessed are you." He begins with a promise, an encouragement, opening up a perspective of hope.

He calls this perspective the "reign of God." The central message of Jesus rings out as "The kingdom of God has come near" (Mark 1:15). With this message of the coming reign of God, Jesus takes up the founding hope of the Old Testament and of people of all times: a longing for peace and freedom, for justice, for love and reconciliation. Jesus affirms this hope against all appearances, and he says why it is true: God himself, God alone guarantees that in the history of the world it is not egoism and the struggle of interests, not cowardly conformity and brutal violence, not lies and deceit, but much more justice and truth, peace and freedom, love and compassion that have the last word.

The Beatitudes are the unfolding of the good news. They show how Jesus's preaching throws our normal standards overboard. It is not the rich, the powerful, the contented, those successful in the world, and the violent who are blessed. Blessed instead are the poor, those who mourn, the meek, and the peacemakers. The kingdom of heaven belongs to them. Blessed are human beings with empty hands. God loves them in a special way. For they are able to receive gifts; they do not stand in God's way. They rely on and trust in God alone; they are open to God's will and call in their lives. They emulate the way in which God acts in history: without violence, hidden, making peace, and seeking to reconcile.

God needs human beings who are generous enough to entrust themselves to this message, who are ready to become witnesses and instruments of hope, who dedicate themselves to seeking justice without violence and to working for peace. Not least of all, God needs people of prayer who pray unceasingly, "Your kingdom come." Ultimately, only those who pray will succeed in fending off the menacing sword hanging over us and in opening a way for reconciliation.

SALT OF THE EARTH, LIGHT OF THE WORLD (FIFTH SUNDAY IN ORDINARY TIME, YEAR A: MATTHEW 5:13–16)

The Gospel describes the mission of the church with the help of three striking images: salt of the earth, light of the world, and a city on the mountain (see Matt 5:13–16).

We flinch involuntarily when we hear these words. Can we really be that—salt of the earth, light of the world? Isn't thinking of ourselves in this way a kind of hopeless overconfidence, and wouldn't it put impossible demands on us? Should we even want to be these things? Isn't such a claim elitist, intolerant, and arrogant?

But the Gospel allows us no escape. It does not say, You should be or shall be the salt of the earth, the light of the world. It says completely clearly and unmistakably, You are salt of the earth and the light of the world, whether or not you want to be. You are it, because you have been enlightened by the light that is God himself and that in Jesus Christ has appeared in the nighttime of our world. And this light of the world that is Jesus Christ has touched not only you. It is not your private property; it belongs to all, and wants to enlighten all.

Today, in particular, we need this salt of the earth. Salt preserves from decay and corruption; it gives flavor and spice. And isn't it true, precisely in our day, that much is beginning to crumble and become lost, that many of our deepest values are being challenged and that this has left wounds and injuries in the hearts of many people? We need the healing power of the gospel in this situation. And, likewise, don't we now often lack light, that is, meaning and direction? And do we not just now need the meaning and purpose that is founded in and emanates from the gospel, and that helps us better understand our world and our lives? Finally, in our situation today—when so many persons have become homeless both externally and internally, and when so many no longer have goals for their lives—do we not also need a "city on the hill" that gives us a sense of orientation, communicates hope, and conveys a sense of home to us?

The Gospel says that the church is a lamp on a lampstand, a city on the hill, and that it must not place its own light under a bushel basket. It must have the courage to be engaged in the world and for the sake of the world. It must not hold itself back—including from the great intellectual challenges of our day.

The church is not here for its own sake, but for the world and for human beings. We have to contextualize this statement about the church as light within the whole of the gospel. For the gospel teaches us that, in letting its light shine, the church has no desire for self-promotion or for building its own image. It should let its light shine so that people "may see your good works and give glory to your Father in heaven" (Matt 5:16). The ultimate purpose and goal of the church is the praise and glory of God, thanksgiving, the celebration of the Eucharist.

"If You Say So…"
(Fifth Sunday in Ordinary Time, Year C: Luke 5:1–11)

"Put out into the deep water," Jesus says to Simon Peter (Luke 5:4–7). It is the challenge not to rest satisfied with what we have achieved.

We must pass on what we have received as a gift. A gift is also a duty.[3]

"If you say so" (Luke 5:5), responds Peter, and he lets out the nets again. Any sensible fisherman would have said, There is no point to it. You're crazy. You simply don't know what you're talking about. You are no expert, no professional. There is no use at this time of the day. But Peter leaves all his human experience behind. He entrusts himself completely to the word of Jesus, and goes out deeper based on Jesus's word. Because *he* said it, Peter sets out trusting that Jesus would make happen what he himself is incapable of doing by his own lights.

We often fail because we rely solely on super-intelligent human analysis and forecasts, and because we think we are obliged to do everything on our own. We often then plunge ourselves into an inhuman activism, one that kills not only the body but also the soul and that more often repels than attracts others. Perhaps that is precisely why there is often such humorlessness and awkwardness in our church. Jesus says also to us, You do not have to do everything with your own power. Trust in God. And trust in my word. That's what is important. That's faith. God is full of wonder, and we can expect miracles from him.

The word of Jesus is both an encouragement and a demand at the same time. It frees us from the pressures of false drivenness. Yet we are also called to take the plunge and entrust ourselves confidently to Jesus. We are called to be the church, to live and act from a deep faith, to be a church that counts on God, takes God seriously, and embraces God.

On the word of Jesus, Simon Peter entrusted himself to God. And he made a miraculous catch. Yet for the evangelist Luke this miracle on the Sea of Galilee is simply an image of an even more miraculous catch, the success of the mission of the young church. For within a generation there were Christian communities in all the great cities on the Mediterranean Sea. This all happened without an organization and infrastructure, simply through a handful of fishermen who had neither special training nor money and social prestige. It happened in the face of overwhelming competition from other religious movements and of the bitter opposition of the Roman state power. The net of this community became so full that it was in danger of breaking.

Jesus has also called us to be "fishers of persons." "Catching" human beings: on first impressions that is no good thing. It sounds like forced conversions. It sounds like enticements, buying and selling, building up our own team. But that does not correspond to the spirit of Jesus. In its deepest sense, faith is a free human act. One only wins the hearts of human beings through the power of conviction. To be a fisher of persons in Jesus's sense means to be a witness—to be witnesses to the freedom for which Jesus Christ has freed us, witnesses to the joy, hope, trust, and courage—to which the good news of the gospel is able to awaken us. Witnesses to the mercy and reconciliation on which our world depends now as much as ever.

"I Say to You, Stand Up" (Seventh Sunday in Ordinary Time, Year B: Mark 2:1–12)

This is a word of both encouragement and admonition. It is God's own word to us. For God has created us upright, in distinction to every other form of life. We can and we should stand up, showing our faces. Each and every one of us has a unique dignity and value. All of us are created in the image of God.

God has shown us in Jesus just how serious he is about this. With his good news of the coming reign of God, Jesus has given particular courage to the poor, the sick, the little, and the weak. Radically, he gave up his life for all and accepted death as the representative of all of us. For God has said in Jesus, and in him in a particular way, "I say to you, stand up" (Mark 2:11). God raised Jesus from the dead. And God will do for us what God has already done for Jesus. Each and every one of us has an eternal future with God.

In raising Jesus from the dead, God showed that the last words are justice and love, not hate and violence; truth and not lies. God showed that in the end life is victorious over the powers of death. God himself will ensure that the violent will not rule forever; God will silence the liars, those who twist the truth. God will lift up the lowly from dust and ashes and will cast the powerful from their thrones. God is the friend of life and will vindicate life.

"I say to you, stand up." These words call out to us today. As Christians, we have every reason to stand up and show our colors. Where there is so much discouragement and hopelessness, we Christians must stand up and say, not only say but demonstrate and set an example, that it makes sense to live, that it makes sense to live well, that it makes sense to live actively in support of what is good, that it makes sense to do good with our lives. If we don't, who will?

"I say to you, stand up." It is not always easy to answer this call. But it is Jesus who is calling, and whatever he calls us to, he makes possible for us to do. Trusting in him we can stand up; because of Jesus, we need have no fear in taking the necessary steps. He is at our side; he offers us his hand; he is our companion and friend. He heals our infirmities and pardons our sins and our weakness. With him, whenever we are "down," we may stand up again each and every day.

MARTHA AND MARY
(SIXTEENTH SUNDAY IN ORDINARY TIME, YEAR C: LUKE 10:38–42)

The Gospel of Luke is the first to introduce Martha to us. She is a thoroughly likeable woman with whom we feel at home and whose guest we would feel honored to be. She does not think first of herself; she cares for her guest and does everything to make Jesus's stay in her home as comfortable as possible. She plunges into all sorts of activities. It is very different with her sister Mary. She also turns completely to Jesus. But she leaves work aside, forgetting her everyday cares for a couple of hours; she sits at Jesus's feet and simply listens to him.

Since the time of the church fathers, the difference between Martha and Mary has been understood as the difference between an active, transactional life and a religious, contemplative life. Especially in the Middle Ages, those in religious life interpreted the words of Jesus about Mary choosing the better part to indicate the superiority of the contemplative life over the active life. But in the gospel story, there is nothing about such a competitive distinction between different forms of life, and no distinction at all between Christians in the world and those in religious life. The contrast pointed out in this story aims in another direction. It is about the difference between the many things that can and must be done by us and the one, essential thing.

Martha cares for her guest. What she does is in no way meaningless or in any way wrong. The tasks of everyday life are essential, and we can never be grateful enough when someone helps us with them. We would be in a bad way if there were no such Marthas in the world. But in her concern for this and that, Martha forgets the most important, even decisive thing. She has no time for what Jesus really wants, and is unable to hear what he wants to share with her. In contrast, Mary is all ears. She not only cares in an outward way for Jesus, but wants simply to be near him and with him; she enjoys the benefit of his company. She lets his comforting and healing words about God and God's coming speak to her. She knows this: as important and right as everything else is, one must not forget the most important thing, the thing on which our life and our life's happiness most depends. "Strive first for the kingdom of God...and all these [other] things will be given to you as well" (Matt 6:33). The one thing must not at all be played off against the other. But we must ask ourselves, What is really necessary?

This gospel story poses a question to us about the meaning of all our doing, of our daily work, our cares and concerns. All too often they eat us alive. Out of concern for our own well-being and that of others, as legitimate as that concern is, we are often enough in danger of losing our souls. We fall into stress and hectic activity because we take little time and leisure to reflect: What is all this actually for? Why am I on earth?

"You are worried and distracted by many things, but there is need of only one thing" (Luke 10:41–42). This sentence does not question the value and necessity of all our concerns. But it does open our eyes to the fact that these concerns can take our attention away from what is essential, from the truth that God is with us. Every moment of our lives is received from God's hand. We are to take joy in God's presence. We are to commend all our actions to God. We are to carry it all to God: our joys and sorrows, hopes and fears, our failures, too, even our difficulties with God, our doubts and our disbelief. We need only turn to God and open ourselves to him.

The assurance of being embraced by God's love and care is liberating, because it also accepts what is partial and incomplete. It gives birth to the hope that God will complete what we ourselves are unable to bring to fulfillment. For faith does not merely remain focused on what is. Rather, it frees us for new action. It frees us for action that builds not only on our own efforts: it derives its power from the presence and power and wisdom of God.

A TREASURE BURIED IN A FIELD (SEVENTEENTH SUNDAY IN ORDINARY TIME, YEAR A: MATTHEW 13:44–52)

The parables of the hidden treasure and of the pearl of great value appear in Matthew's Gospel (chapter 13). Jesus speaks of a worker and a pearl merchant. Both have improbable luck. They each make *the* great discovery of their lives! The merchant finds a pearl of great value. The day laborer discovers a treasure either while grave digging or while plowing in his employer's field. According to existing law, he would have been required to hand over his discovered treasure to the owner of the land. But it does not happen this way in the parable. The parable evokes a longing that is hidden deep in every human being: the desire for fortune. In their search for happiness, both men, the merchant and the day laborer, discover *the* great prize of their lives. But when the opportunity to make one's fortune arises, the moment must be seized, cost what it may. "In his joy," says the text, "he goes and sells all that he has and buys that field" (Matt 13:44). In his joy he seeks his fortune with both hands.

It is just this way with the kingdom of heaven, says Jesus. He is the treasure in the field. He is the pearl of great value, the lucky find, the chance of a lifetime. In Jesus's coming there also comes the singular opportunity to gain salvation, the kingdom of heaven.

This treasure is the kingdom of heaven, the reign of God. Jesus himself and the New Testament describe it with many other images: life, justice, peace, freedom. The theological tradition says simply *beatitudo*, "blessedness."

It comes down to seeking this pearl of great value, this hidden treasure, that has been given to us, to recognizing it, lifting it out of the dust and dirt that had settled onto it over time, and bringing it to light again.

The treasure was found in the field; the pearl was discovered while the merchant worked. Field and work, they are the realms of daily life. They stand, above all, for the cares and challenges of daily life. Here, hidden in the midst of the "daily grind," in the field of our day-to-day responsibilities, is where the treasure is to be found. That is the promise of Jesus.

The answer to the deepest longings of human beings is very clear: the gospel, the good news of Jesus Christ, is our treasure, our pearl. Whoever has found these belongs among

51

the blessed ones. Such a person has everything she longs for: joy, security, life—the fullness of life.

Heaven is where the glory of God comes completely and permanently upon us human beings. Heaven is the gift of the most intimate and personal communion with God, who alone can fulfill and satisfy us.

Let us seek out times of silence, of prayer, and of spiritual renewal over and over again. They are no flight from reality; rather, they are the willingness to enter ever more deeply into the world, to plow ever deeper to find the treasure.

This great discovery and this great happiness cannot be "made." They must be received as a gift. But there is one thing we can do: we can ready ourselves to give up everything, if necessary, for the sake of this one thing, the reign of God. The Bible calls such readiness *metanoia*. It may seem difficult to us. But the parable says to us that this *metanoia*, this letting go, brings us "full joy."

"I DESIRE MERCY" (EIGHTEENTH SUNDAY IN ORDINARY TIME, YEAR A: MATTHEW 14:13–21)

"When Jesus heard that John had been beheaded…." (see Matt 14:13). John the Baptist had to pay with his life for his support of the cause of God and the commandments of God. Because he had spoken the truth directly to the envious and lustful Herod, John was thrown into jail and then lost his head. The first public appearance of Jesus follows on this catastrophe. And it is very probable that Jesus foresaw his own fate in the fate of the Baptist, his own violent death on the cross as a consequence of this public appearance.

Jesus does not give up in response to the death of the Baptist. He does not give up, because he has compassion for people—especially for the sick, the weak, and the poor. And, as we are told next, he does not leave the weary and hungry simply sitting there in the desert. He does not send them away, but befriends them and asks his disciples to do the same. The basic posture of Jesus, and of those committed to following him, is an existence for others. And so, he says to his disciples, "You give them something to eat" (Matt 14:16).

There, standing in front of their eyes, are real people: children, youth, families, the elderly, the sick. They need physical help; they also have hunger and thirst in their souls. They carry physical and often also emotional wounds around with them.

Our world can be so unmerciful. Often everything is tied down into structures, laws, and anonymous procedures. The individual human being in her particular and unique situation does not matter. But people want to be accepted personally. In a world of increasing individualism, even of selfishness and declining solidarity where everyone is only out for himself, many are looking for human beings who perceive the suffering of others and allow themselves to be affected by it. We need a new culture of mercy.

The people of God, in both the Old and New Testaments, lived by remembering and retelling stories of the mercy of God, as the Bible tells us. They needed to hear again and again "Be merciful, just as your Father is merciful" (Luke 6:36).

Doesn't progress have a downside, in that it destroys many human values and relationships? We feel the need for a turn to a new beginning, a deeper reality. The need for religious support and consolation, the need for mercy has arisen again.

We can do nothing by ourselves and of our own power. But if we bring the little that we have to God, put it into his hand and place it at his disposal, then there is enough for all as we receive it back from God's hand.

SEASONS OF GRACE

In the reign of God nothing is measured according to quantitative criteria. God can make much of the little that we bring. God can make it that all are satisfied. We receive what is most essential in our lives as a gift.

THE STORM ON THE SEA
(NINETEENTH SUNDAY IN ORDINARY TIME,
YEAR A: MATTHEW 14:22–33)

The gospel account of the storm on the sea and of Jesus walking on the stormy sea (see Matt 14:22–33) expresses very vividly what faith can and must mean for every Christian: faith is overcoming fear through trust in the God of Jesus Christ.

Fear lurks at the bottom of our soul. For risking one's life in freedom and in one's own responsibility means going out on the high seas. No one has control over the future. To live means facing the abyss; life is full of surprises and pitfalls, threatened by death. It follows that, for the one who lives by faith and grounds her very existence in faith, there are no railings guaranteeing her safety in the water. We cannot see God and straightforwardly prove God's existence. Waves often crash against the boat of the church, so that the believers are shaken vigorously back and forth. Often, we must row without apparent success against the winds and must believe in the face of the ill currents of our own day.

Yet this is not only true today; it has been so from the very beginning, and is the fundamental situation of the church. In just this way the earliest disciples overcame fear and terror. Even Peter was filled with fear and, to the extent that he gave into it, he risked sinking into the sea. He only found security by entrusting himself to the words of Jesus: "Take heart, it is

I; do not be afraid!" (Matt 14:27).[4] The outstretched hand of Jesus caught him and rescued him.

And so it is with us: trusting in Jesus means leaving the seemingly safe boat, giving up on false promises and assurances (which, at any rate, are not reliable in an emergency), and making God, our one truly reliable support, the foundation of our lives. "My help comes from the LORD, who made heaven and earth" (Ps 121:2).

Every one of us will be challenged again and again by doubt on this path of faith. In German, the word for doubt carries the literal sense of someone keeping two scenarios, two possibilities in mind at the same time, of someone looking in two directions and not only in one.[5] We tend to want to have it two ways at the same time, to have a foot in both camps. To decide in favor of faith is to be like Peter and reach only toward Jesus Christ.

Jesus's call, "Come," determines our only possible direction (see Matt 14:29).

Such trusting faith, faith that is able to overcome our small-heartedness and lack of courage, calls for largeness of heart, the courage for great things. In order really to live, to gain a large and wide perspective, we have to clear much away, give much up, let it go, and so become able to see what had obscured our vision and blocked our path. If we only want to have and to consume more, we will miss our chance to *be* more. Jesus gives us courage to set out on the good and ultimately only practical way, even if this way seems at the time to be a risky one, a more difficult one, a way calling for personal sacrifices. "Come." This call of the Lord goes out to every Christian. Whoever hears this call—in prayer, from our fellow human beings, or in our daily lives—walks on water and passes over the abyss.

Enduring the Headwinds
(Nineteenth Sunday in Ordinary Time,
Year A: Matthew 14:22–33)

Sometimes we feel as if the waves are crashing over us and that we have no firm ground under our feet. No human being and above all no Christian can expect to be spared from such experiences. Headwinds, as the gospels tell us in many places, are an inescapable part of Christian existence.

So, we should not be shocked or even surprised when a headwind comes up and blows coldly in our face. Should we really expect that it will go better for us than it went for the disciples and friends of Jesus? Dare we imagine it going better for us than for our master, who, humanly speaking, failed on the cross—even if he really did ultimately triumph?

The gospel story of the storm on the sea gives a response to this question. It is an unusual and striking response. The frightened disciples do not react to the danger by plunging into a frantic attempt to bail water out of the boat. What could they accomplish with their weak strength and limited means in the face of such gigantic waves? They also do not try to save their lives by recklessly tossing real and imagined ballast overboard. Such a move would have left the boat weightless and quite helpless in the face of the waves. A ship can ride out a storm only if it has a deep keel and, through its own weight, does not ride at the surface but reaches firmly into the depths.

The frightened disciples call out, even cry out to the Lord. He and only he can help them in their distress. And so they trust and rely on him. For even the wind and the sea obey him. Everything was created in him and through him, the One come from eternity. By his death and resurrection he has conquered all powers of evil and of death. He is the Lord and head of his church. He steers and guides it, and always remains with it. He is the one who travels with us in the boat of our own lives.

Let us call out and pray to him! Let us pray often, regularly, and sincerely! Then the sea storm that is in us ourselves will subside, and a great calm will enter into us.

We need human beings who live from this silence and from their faith, and who therefore are not afraid; human beings who have defeated the waves and swells of egoism, and who are thus able to comfort others when there is a storm; human beings who, through friendship with Jesus Christ, are friends to others and thus bring about more friendship, peace, and reconciliation. We need human beings who awaken and pray at night, human beings who keep searching for signs of the coming reign of God, and human beings who witness to God's healing presence in word and deed.

Remaining Faithful (Nineteenth Sunday in Ordinary Time, Year C: Luke 12:32–48)

The gospel story of the faithful and the unfaithful servants is one of Jesus's judgment discourses. Here Jesus tells us, Do not be deceived and do not lull yourself into a false sense of security. In the end, all of you must give an account of your actions. There can be no playacting or hiding, for all masks will fall away. For all of you will be asked whether you have been faithful and wise, just as the servant in the gospel was asked.

Only at first glance can this gospel story be understood as wanting to scare us and fill us with fear and terror of eternal damnation. In reality, this story is not a threatening message but good news. In parable form it shows us what great trust God has placed in us human beings. God appoints us as stewards of the goods of this earth, and thus passes on to us the responsibility to care for nature and especially for our fellow human beings. Thus, God entrusts something to us. God confers responsibility on us. The well-being or grief of the world, the preservation or destruction of creation, peace or war and violence among human beings: God has entrusted all this into our hands. We are largely the shapers of our own happiness. The human being can shape his life well, making something of it; or, through his own fault, he can also mess up his life, fritter it away, and waste it. God loves us precisely as free creatures. God recognizes our dignity as human beings.

There is nothing that a human being can so misuse as her own freedom. And therein our contemporary problem actually lies. We can do with our lives just what the unfaithful servant of the gospel did. He shamelessly exploited and abused the freedom and trust placed in him. He lived riotously, feasting and drinking, but harassing and abusing others; he became violent toward them and denied them their rightful wages. He did not grasp that freedom does not entail despotism but responsibility.

The lesson of the faithful and unfaithful servant is this: Do not lull yourself into false security. In the end, all of you must give an account of your actions. There are limits that we must respect. For, in the end, we will all stand before the same judge, before whom all are finally equal and are judged by the same standard. This, too, is good news.

This means that lies and violence do not have the last word, but truth and justice do. The really wise person is not the one who knows every trick in the book and operates with cunning and shrewdness and clever tricks, throwing his elbows around as much as possible. The wise person is the one who reckons with the reality of God in her life, gratefully acknowledging what God has entrusted to her and handling it responsibly—always ready to give an accounting of herself.

In the end, we will be asked by God about our own personal

responsibility. We will be asked, Have you been reliable and faithful, decent, sincere, and straightforward; have you shown backbone and strength of character; were you a rock and a tower of strength in the storm? Or were you a broken reed, allowing yourself to be blown back and forth by rapidly changing fashions and opinions of the day, living according to every whim? In short, have you acted and lived according to your conscience, or have you allowed yourself to drift and acted only according to the motto: You shall not let yourself get caught? Were you the true and faithful servant in the gospel who was praised and rewarded?

Faithfulness remains important today in a particular way. For, according to the scriptures, faithfulness is the basic characteristic of God. We hear it again and again: God is ever faithful. God is faithful even when we are not. God does not let us fall, not a single one of us. We can rely unconditionally on God, and ultimately only on God. We can trust God in any situation. God is our refuge and our strength, our fortress and our rock. We can count on God, and to him we must also give an accounting of our life.

If God is so unwaveringly faithful to us, then we too must be faithful and found to be faithful in all things. Our credibility as Christians depends on this, namely, that we can be depended on, that we can be trusted, that we are true and faithful servants, that we live and act from inner responsibility. Like love, freedom must prove itself in faithfulness.

INNER AND OUTER TRUTHFULNESS (TWENTY-SECOND SUNDAY IN ORDINARY TIME, YEAR B: MARK 7:1–8, 14–15, 21–23)

Jesus wants to draw attention away from what is external and focus on what is essential, the internal. "There is nothing outside a person that by going in can defile, but the things that come out are what defile" (Mark 7:15). What a person thinks, says, and does, what she presents to the external world, all comes down to what is inside her.

The distinction that Jesus makes in the gospel between "clean" and "unclean" was very important for the people of Israel. Those who wanted communion with God had to do something for it. They had to stay away from anything that would not be pleasing to God—for example, from animals that people of other religions had sacrificed to their gods. They had to stay away from people who had committed a crime, from lepers, from the dead, and from much more. Contact with "unclean" things or people made the faithful Jews themselves unclean. If someone then wanted to come back into relationship with God, he had to purify himself externally by washing or a purification offering.

In no way did Jesus want to do away with or destroy the religious laws and traditions. He was concerned with the true meaning, the original spirit of such laws: a person should do God's will with her whole heart and inner commitment. If she does so, then the cleaning of hands after contact with "impure" things or people is quite secondary. Jesus is concerned with purity of heart. Here is where a person is either good or evil, as are also his actions. The external offering must be an expression of an interior devotion of the heart; otherwise it is mere formality or even idolatry. For Jesus, what matters is the truthfulness and integrity of our actions.

The church, too, is repeatedly called to review its traditional forms, habits, and customs. Are they still filled with their original spirit, or have they become hollow and superficial? For example, let's look at the rich liturgy of the church. Our magnificent liturgical rites and rubrics are in danger of becoming empty and external rituals if we do not internalize them anew and so make them spiritually fruitful.

Traditions that were once truly helpful can block what really matters, if one keeps them alive merely for their own sake. We have an example in the still ongoing controversies around receiving communion by hand or by mouth. External forms are being argued over, with some persons even demonizing each other (and so forgetting the main commandment of love of neighbor!). But what is decisive is reverence for the sacrament—and that can be expressed either way, just as it can be missing either way! Our interior attitudes are what matter.

Still, we must bring into the external world whatever we have internalized and recognized as good; it must become our action. Seen in this way, it is not only the inner attitude that is essential, but also the external deed. What is external also matters, but not in the sense of mere outer forms, as in public displays of a luxurious lifestyle or in lavish promises. Much more, our exterior actions and affairs must mirror our inner attitudes. It must be clear from our exterior actions that we are people who have decided to do God's will with our whole hearts and that we want to devote ourselves to others through works of love. The truth wants to be done. Otherwise our inner dispositions would be as untruthful as our purely external actions. It is a matter of both internal and external integrity.

Being Open to God's Word (Twenty-Third Sunday in Ordinary Time, Year B: Mark 7:31–37)

The deaf-mute man in today's Gospel, to whom Jesus gives all his attention and healing presence and whom he thus frees from his illness, is an image for our present situation. The deaf man's inability to hear his fellow human beings, and thus his inability to share their sorrows and joys, is reminiscent of a situation that is far too prevalent in our society: we live past each other; we are so busy with our own concerns that we have no time for what others have to say to us. Although we have healthy ears, we are often spiritually deaf—deaf to our environment and also deaf to the call of God.

At the same time, we are impaired of speech. Although most of us are very skillful at "making words," our words are often empty. Haven't many of the words that we exchange in our conversations become little more than meaningless phrases? Often enough we are in the paradoxical situation of being "mute" in the midst of an elaborate conversation, closed in on ourselves, alone with our own feelings and anxieties that we either cannot or dare not express.

Jesus is savior also in our contemporary situation. He heals the deaf-mute man by saying to him, "Ephphatha—be opened" (Mark 7:34). Jesus knows that we human beings can only live rightly when we live in relationship with one another. So, he wants to open us to one another and thus further heal our human relationships. God himself is a God-in-relationship. The miracle thus takes place within the relationship with God the Father: the deaf-mute man can hear and see.

Already in the writings of the church fathers, this deaf-mute man became an image of the unredeemed human being, closed and crippled within himself, unable to hear the Word of God or to pass on faith to others. This deafness und dumbness are the mark of our own time. Jesus must touch us, sharing with us something of his own power and spirit, so that we become able to receive and understand salvation, and to witness to it by our lives.

We are called to go out to others, as Jesus did, and say to them, Have confidence, I'll stretch out my hand, I offer my love. Leave the small shell of your loneliness, and "open" yourself. Please tell me what moves you and torments you. I accept you. And even more than I do, so does God accept you. God frees you from all the fetters that both you and others have made for you. God hears you, and you may speak to him.

KEEPING DOORS OPEN (TWENTY-FOURTH SUNDAY IN ORDINARY TIME, YEAR C: LUKE 15:1–32)

The parable of the return of the prodigal son shows us family life not as a refuge or an island of the blessed, but quite realistically as a place of manifold everyday conflicts. It tells us of a father who must undergo the painful experience of his younger son suddenly freaking out and taking off for a lifestyle not entirely acceptable to the father. Many parents face such experiences in our world today. Over and over again, they have to let go of their children at different ages. Parents must do this for their children to become independent. But it also hurts; and if their children do go their own way, many wonder whether they have done something wrong.

It is amazing just how much the Gospel holds back in its judgment here. It neither praises the one who remains home nor even less—and this is truly amazing—condemns the one who leaves and then comes back again. The father does not preach to him, makes no accusations against him, does not disinherit him, and certainly does not show him the door. On the contrary, he holds the door open. The father keeps a lookout for him, he goes to meet him, and seeks him out; he receives him with open arms, restores him to his full rights as a son, and even organizes a family reunion celebration for him.

The disappointment of the son who remained at home is understandable. But not only the son who was initially lost must repent and go home; the other, well-behaved one who stayed home must change his mind and learn something. He must learn to drop his jealousy, self-righteousness, and hard-heartedness; he must become merciful and reopen the doors of the home and of his heart to his brother.[6]

This story can show us that families should constitute a house with open doors; not a house in which children can remain forever, but one to which they may always return. One could also put it this way: The family should constitute a realm in which all members are accepted, where all respect one another and try to understand one another, where members share with one another and talk openly to one another; where they help one another and stand up for one another; where they forgive one another and are happy to be together with one another. Therefore, families must have not only open doors, but eyes, ears, hands, and hearts that are open for one another.

Jesus says to us in the gospel, Look at how God behaves toward you; how God forgives you and accepts you again and again despite all your weaknesses and sins. You should behave in this same way. In your marital and family life, you ought to be a mirror of the way God acts toward you. Spouses should help each other experience something of the love and unconditional fidelity of God in their tenderness, love, fidelity, respect, and helpfulness for each other.

Only the one who knows about the kind Father in heaven, who is oriented to God and his example, who knows that she and all others are accepted and sustained by God, that she is lifted up by God in good days and bad, who knows that he lives from and with God; only such a person has the strength to continue living as God wants us to live, even in the midst of the difficulties and crises that come upon all marriages and families. For we are simply not able to do this by our own strength.

We are able to hold doors open to one another only to

the extent that we again and again open doors and windows upward, upward toward God our Father in heaven. A Catholic Christian who wants to keep the doors of his heart open will certainly also be open to the teaching of the church; he cannot simply write it off. Yet, if he has honestly opened himself to it, then he can and must decide according to his personal conscience. Above all, he should know this: like a kind father, God always holds the doors of his heart open to us—always filled with understanding and ready to forgive.

"WHOEVER WISHES TO BE FIRST" (TWENTY-FIFTH SUNDAY IN ORDINARY TIME, YEAR B: MARK 9:30–37)

Jesus takes his disciples aside by themselves. The crowds that had initially been streaming jubilantly to Jesus have now withdrawn from him; only a small company of disciples is left. As the opposition to him is forming, all the more intensively Jesus teaches his disciples.

The reign of God is not concerned with quantity; instead it is all about quality!

In what does God's reign consist? The Gospel gives us a response that is, at first glance, shocking, even scandalous. The Son of Man will be betrayed into human hands, he will be killed, and after three days he will rise again (see Mark 9:31). For the Apostle Paul, too, the death and resurrection of Jesus Christ is the exact center of the Christian message and the core of the good news. That sounds strange, but it is very liberating, truly good news.

That Jesus was handed over to death on the cross means that the God whom we confess as Christians is not enthroned far away above the clouds, beyond all the horrors and hardships of history. Our God is a God of human beings who has freely entered into our human fate. He was born as a small, weak child, suffered hunger and thirst, and experienced human friendship—but also human hatred, resentment, and betrayal. This God entered into suffering and death, even dying the most shameful death imaginable in the ancient world, death on the gallows of the cross. Nothing human remains distant from this God. Since then there can be no human situation, however bad and however muddled, that is fundamentally godless and profane. In everything and in all situations, God is close to us. In all situations, God accepts us. Christian faith sees and accepts not only our strengths; it values not only our heroism. Christian faith sees and values our human weakness, lowliness, and misery.

But faith does not stop here. It transfigures our misery, suffering, and dying. God does not desire death, but life. And so, God did not leave Jesus in death but raised him to new and eternal life. God did not hand life over to death, truth to lies, justice and love to hatred and violence. Therefore, the Christian message is a message of hope. It gives us courage to live and act. It tells us that it is never useless to search for and do what is good. For goodness will conquer in the end.

From this central message, the Gospel now draws a central consequence: "Whoever wants to be first must be last of all and servant of all" (Mark 9:35). Again, we do not initially want to hear words such as these. They seem to call for false humility and spinelessness. But what is intended is that we Christians are not meant to be the kind of people who dominate others or are dominated by others; we are not meant to be people who are only or primarily in it for ourselves, but people who are there for others. These words radically contradict all egoism that seeks only self-assertion, self-accomplishment, and self-actualization—and these at others' expense. These words thus call on a different experience, one that we have all had. For we really are happy when we help others be happy.

And so, Jesus calls us to goodness, gentleness, helpfulness, virtue, friendliness. And in doing so he tells us how one recognizes a true Christian: not in pious posturing, but in love of neighbor and concern for others.

THE CHILD AS SIGN
(TWENTY-FIFTH SUNDAY IN ORDINARY TIME, YEAR B: MARK 9:29–36)

In the Gospel, Jesus says, "Whoever wants to be the first must be last of all and servant of all" (Mark 9:35). Jesus in no way means that we should forget who we are, declining to use our skills and talents and thus squandering these talents. What he does mean is that no one may seek to develop and use his abilities and talents at the expense of others. Rather, we are to use our gifts for the common good and to assume responsibility for all together.

With respect to our image of human beings, what matters is having the right Christian image, one stamped by the light of Jesus Christ. To make this point clearly and concretely visible, in the Gospel Jesus places a child in the midst of the disciples. The child is at the center as the central figure. What is Jesus's point here? He is making clear that a human society, if it is to be truly human in service of humanity, must also be a society that welcomes children.

And in placing a child at the center in today's Gospel, Jesus is making another, deeper point. The child is also a symbol for us as adults. A child is without power, dependent on the help of parents and other adults. Jesus thus wants to draw attention to this: you, adults, you too ultimately remain dependent in your lives. All of you are as dependent on your heavenly Father as children are. Jesus is exhorting us to rediscover our own childhood before God.

It is a matter of the "spirit of adoption." That is, ultimately every single one of us can only receive our life as a gift from God. We are thus allowed to remain weak and unfinished and small before God, like children. We do not need constantly to prove ourselves, either to ourselves or to others through our accomplishments. We are accepted, affirmed, and loved. Before God we all have an infinite value and dignity. We can be confident in God, because God holds us and sustains us. We may cast our anxieties before God. Humanity is the way of the church. The church wants to serve human beings and show them the way to a successful human life, a success that finds its purpose and fulfillment only in God. The church wants to accompany all of us, to make the journey with us so that we advance toward this goal. Let us remain human beings who are on the way, and let us constantly renew ourselves along this way to God. God walks with us, God is with us.

JESUS AND THE CHILDREN (TWENTY-EIGHTH SUNDAY IN ORDINARY TIME, YEAR B: MARK 10:17–30)

How did Jesus act toward children? What does he have to say to us for our conduct along the way? In this matter, as in others, Jesus's conduct is frankly revolutionary. He gives us a radical alternative. There is an unambiguous instance of this in the Gospel of Mark (see 10:13–16). We are told there that people were bringing little children to Jesus that he might touch them. But the disciples dismissed the people harshly and pushed the children aside. Children were not greatly valued at the time; like women, they were not taken seriously. Children were only important as future adults; that is, they would be a source of offspring and support in their parents' old age. Jesus sets himself in opposition to such a stance; he is downright indignant about the conduct of his disciples: "Let the little children come to me…for it is to such as these that the kingdom of God belongs" (Mark 9:14). On another occasion, Jesus places a child front and center, making her the key figure: "Whoever welcomes one such child in my name welcomes me" (Mark 9:37).

Children are the first candidates for the reign of God, as they are also Jesus's representatives. Children stand under his special protection (see Mark 10:14). For Jesus, prestige, performance, success, and practical advantage count for nothing. They are not the true measure of our humanity. Jesus turns our normal scale of values upside down. He has a preference for the poor, weak, oppressed, sick—and for children: "Truly, I tell you, whoever does not receive the kingdom of God as a little child will never enter it" (Mark 10:15).

Before God, our heavenly Father, all of us are and remain children. Being a child is decisive for adults and not vice versa.

As a matter of fact, we grownups have much to learn from children. Children enrich us, are fun to be with, and lift our spirits. Children can bombard us with questions and can teach us that nothing is self-evident. They give us food for thought, questions, and reasons to be amazed. The cheerfulness, informality, spontaneity, and creativity of children can be contagious. Children want to be held, to love, and be loved; they bring warmth into our modern frigidity. Children can speak the truth without guile, holding up a mirror for us. Last but not least, children are naturally religious; in their own way, they ask ultimate questions and know that we are not capable of making everything happen, that life is ultimately a gift. This is what Jesus means when he says that we must become like children. We must relearn to experience everything as a gift.

If, in spite of everything, adolescents go their own way and distance themselves from the church, then it is no help to try to coerce or scold them, and no help at all to break off contact with them. The critical questions of adolescent sons and daughters should rather cause us to think in new and deeper ways about our faith, to grow and mature in it. For children shape our lives, too, and we are never finished growing in our lives. And the ways in which we shape them will be determinative as we all move ahead.

What is important is a future and a child-friendly society in which we reckon with inner values instead of focusing on outer progress, performance, and success. What is important is a society that takes its measure from Jesus Christ, his friendship with humanity and, especially, with children. Such a new society begins in our homes, in our own families. The family is still the basic unit of society and the church. And our future will ultimately be decided in our families—not in parliaments, intergovernmental conferences, or bishops' conferences.

WHAT MUST I DO?
(TWENTY-EIGHTH SUNDAY IN ORDINARY TIME, YEAR B: MARK 10:17–30)

A young man comes to Jesus and asks a question. It is the decisive question in the life of every human being: What must I do to inherit eternal life? It is a fundamental question, one asked by everyone and especially by every young person: What can, should, and must I do so that my life succeeds, so that it brings deep and lasting happiness? How can I gain life?

Human beings not only have this question, we are this question. For, in contrast to every other living being on earth, the human being is entrusted to him- or herself. She can gain her life, but can also lose it. He can gain eternal happiness, but can also lose it.

Jesus gives us a response that is unequivocal and without ambiguity: "No one is good but God alone" (Mark 10:18). The good, fulfilled, successful life consists in nothing and no one except God. God is the good, the supreme good; God alone is the happiness and salvation of human beings. God alone is big enough to fulfill the height and depth, the length and breadth of our longing for life. We human beings are insatiable in our hunger and thirst for life. No earthly good, however good, great, and beautiful, can ultimately satisfy our heart.

And so again the question: What must I do? What is the way to God? Jesus's response is very sobering—nothing at all extraordinary or grandiose. Jesus simply refers to the commandments. They are—as the Psalms tell us again and again—directions, path markers on the way to life. And which of us could say of ourselves, as the rich young man in the Gospel says, that we have always followed these commandments since our childhood? Let us not hastily seek out extraordinary spiritual paths! Let's stick for a while with the tried-and-true bread of Christian living. In the long run, it is healthier and more digestible than the extravagant specialties. One can upset one's stomach religiously, too!

The Gospel reports that Jesus looked at the young man with love. He offered friendship to him. That is what's important. Not additional laws, rules, and methods for the spiritual life. The law of the new covenant is Jesus Christ in person. We are to follow him. For he is the way, the truth, and the life.

Following Jesus is beautiful and fulfilling. Yet it is not easy. It does not take one by the wide path, along which all stroll comfortably. It moves upward along a steep path. It leads one to new life along the way of the cross. It stores up treasure in heaven and not on this earth.

The path to life is one along which we must leave some things and, ultimately, all things behind. "Sell what you own, and give the money to the poor" (Mark 10:21). Those are radical words. We must not minimize or polish away their adamancy and hardness. The one we are following is the crucified One, and we must not try to sneak past the cross.

For the cross is our only hope. It is the only possible way to the new life of Easter and Pentecost. We only become truly free for God and for others by letting go, surrendering, dying again and again. Christian freedom is not gained through rebelliousness, but through surrendering oneself for what is greatest, for the kingdom of heaven and for the sake of human beings. Freedom is realized in this ever-larger love, in self-giving. Such love is the meaning of our lives, the meaning of our world.

"MALE AND FEMALE…"
(TWENTY-NINTH SUNDAY IN ORDINARY TIME, YEAR C: LUKE 18:1–8)

This is the story of a very persistent woman. She is no timid, intimidated "cricket on the hearth."[7] This woman dares to go before a judge "who neither feared God nor had respect for people" (Luke 18:2). Although "only" a widow, she demands of this mighty and even violent judge that he grant her justice against her opponent. He wants to ignore the matter, but the woman does not let up. She keeps demanding, "Grant me justice."

"Grant me justice": this is also the demand of many women in the face of myriad hardships, affronts, and discriminatory practices. They too do not want to be ignored any longer.

What are the fundamentals of church teaching? The first and most basic statement can be found on the first pages of Sacred Scripture. The biblical creation story says clearly, "God created humankind in his image, in the image of God he created them; male and female he created them" (Gen 1:27). The dignity of human beings, of every human being, could not be stated more clearly. And human beings exist only in the "double edition" of male and female, who are mutually dependent. Being in the image of God and being in two sexes thus belong together. Both male and female are the image of God. They are not the same, but they are of equal value and dignity. In the equality of their dignity, they stand in a relationship of partnership.

Woman is the biblical Eve, correctly understood. Not in any negative sense as the "daughter of Eve" as she was too often seen in the history of Christianity—the easily tempted, the weaker sex, the temptress and seducer of the man. No, the biblical image of woman as Eve is of the mother of all the living. In a special way, she is the protector and preserver of life. The vocation of women is the vocation to serve life, not only in the biological sense, but human life in the broadest sense: she is called in a particular way to foster and care for a life in which there is equal space for heart and mind in the midst of so many violent forces.

Jesus preaches the reign of God. In God's reign this original sense of the order of creation is to be reestablished and realized in an unsurpassable way.

This new creation has become reality in the death and resurrection of Jesus Christ. So, it was obvious to Paul that men and women are coequal members of the church. He writes to the Galatians, "There is no longer Jew or Greek, there is no longer slave or free, there is no longer male and female; for all of you are one in Christ Jesus" (Gal 3:28). Before God and in Christ there is no subordination or inferiority of women. There, all differences lose any divisive and discriminatory meaning.

Service of life is equally entrusted to both men and women. And men must grant justice to women; men must honor the equal dignity of women; they must help create conditions in which women can live their vocations in a way worthy of human beings. Not against one another, but only with each other can women and men shape a renewed, truly human world.

LIGHT OF THE WORLD
(THIRTIETH SUNDAY IN ORDINARY TIME, YEAR B: MARK 10:46–52)

The blind beggar Bartimaeus, to whom Jesus gives all his attention and healing presence and thus frees from his illness, is a reflection of our own present situation. The incapacity of this blind man to see his surroundings and his fellow human beings in all of their worries and joys reminds us of a deep distress of our own society. We often live past each other; we are so concerned with ourselves, circling only around ourselves, seeing only as far as our own good and interests. Our view is very often blind to what others want to show or share with us. Even though our eyes are fine, we are in a very real sense blind. Blind to the human beings around us, blind to the signs of the times, blind to the traces of God in our world.

Jesus turns to the blind Bartimaeus and says to him, "Go; your faith has made you well" (Mark 10:52). Jesus gives him eyesight, restores his vision, brings light to his disfigured eyes. In John's Gospel, Jesus says of himself, "I am the light of the world" (John 8:12). Jesus is, so to speak, the means through which reality is genuinely illuminated, fully, in all its height and depth, its length and breadth. Only in him does the full truth of the world and of human beings become evident.

He also heals our blindness. And so, Christian faith, that is, faith in Jesus Christ as the light of the world, does not entail any narrowed-down vision, any ideological blinders, or any small-mindedness. Faith in Jesus Christ is what first frees our vision to see reality in its wholeness and truth. Why is that so? Because everything was created in and through Jesus Christ. He is the archetype and purpose of creation, its Alpha and the Omega, its beginning, middle, and end. So, he is also the light, the key, as it were, and the code for understanding the world in its depth. In him we are told definitively who we are, what the world is, and what it means.

To allow oneself to be embraced by Jesus Christ, and so to become a light and a carrier of light to others: that is our task as the church. To carry the light of faith, the light of the good news out to the peoples of the world, but also in to our own surroundings and workplaces, is the task of all the followers of Jesus. We must remember our religious roots and traditions. As Christians, it is our task to lay the spiritual foundations for a new evangelization, which can bring the light of faith into our contemporary world. Jesus Christ, himself the primary light of the world, also calls us the light of the world, and he adds, "Let your light shine before others, so that they may see your good works and give glory to your Father in heaven" (Matt 5:16).

Standing Up (Monday of the Thirtieth Week in Ordinary Time: Luke 13:10–17)

People can be crippled in various ways. Often it happens through difficult and heavy physical work. Or they can be crippled from sickness, sometimes beginning from childhood.

People can also be crippled or consumed inwardly, having taken a knock. They can be crippled because they are internally broken, having been disappointed, or having tensed up and hidden themselves away. Or they can be crippled because their spirit has been broken—whether by bad upbringing; unjust, humiliating treatment; or oppressive social structures. Finally, many are crippled because they only think of themselves, revolving only in and around themselves, no longer reaching out to others openly or uprightly; they can become closed in and no longer able to find the way out of their egoism. There are many ways in which a human life can become crippled or impaired.

Jesus saw the crippled woman. We hear this again and again in the gospels: Jesus took the suffering and misery of human beings seriously and so was moved by compassion.

Being seen by Jesus is not merely being detected; it is really being seen at heart and taken seriously, being seen by one who is aware that human beings are not meant to be crippled. God has willed and created us differently. God has created human beings in his image and likeness, so that anyone bearing a human countenance radiates something of God's beauty, majesty, and glory. God has bestowed on us a value and dignity that we might walk uprightly.

It is sin that cripples human beings, that humiliates us and turns us back in on ourselves. The sinner is a human being turned in on him- or herself, one who forgets his true happiness and vocation, one who orients herself in false and wrong ways to the things of this world, absolutizing them and revolving only around herself. Such a person is no longer open to God and other human beings. He has lost the meaning of his life.

At the center of today's Gospel, though, is not the crippled woman; at the center is Jesus, savior of human beings. He sees the misery of this woman, takes it seriously, calls her over to himself and says, "Woman, you are set free from your ailment" (Luke 13:12).

The healed woman can now stand upright, look other human beings in the eye, and turn her gaze toward heaven. She is a symbol of holistic pastoral care. Pastoral care should lead persons to an upright stance, giving them back their courage, confidence, worth, and dignity. Pastoral care begins when we say to another, You are someone, you have infinite worth, for God loves you from all eternity, affirms your existence, holds you, and sustains you. You matter because God is crazy about you and wants to live in communion with you forever.

The Gospel tells us clearly what ultimately constitutes upright living: "Immediately she stood up straight and began praising God" (Luke 13:13). The true dignity of human beings consists of praising God. The human being finds her ultimate fulfillment only in praising God. Conversely, the famous saying of Irenaeus of Lyon is also true: "The glory of God is the human being fully alive."

INHERITANCE AND RESPONSIBILITY (THIRTY-THIRD SUNDAY IN ORDINARY TIME, YEAR A: MATTHEW 25:14–30)

The parable of the talents (Matt 25:14–30; Luke 19:11–27) is not at all foreign to our era and our approach to work. We could begin the parable today with these words: "A multi-millionaire flies to the other side of the globe at least once a year, in order to establish a new company there. While he is away, he appoints a number of deputy CEOs. The first is given responsibility for five corporate divisions, and the second for three. A third deputy is to concern himself with a subsidiary corporation. When the CEO returns from his trip and demands an accounting, the first and second deputies not only report a healthy outcome of their work, but are able to report on the significant expansions they had been able to accomplish. The third deputy, however, had done nothing and thus had nothing to report. And his reasoning was this: I don't trust you for even a moment.

According to the parable of Jesus, this third one, the weak one, will be punished severely. Why is that so? Was he lazy? Did Jesus already have in mind a twenty-first century kind of meritocracy that only accepts success? Hardly! For if he did, Jesus himself would never have gone the way of human failure, abandonment, and death on the cross.

This third man of the parable is a key figure in understanding life by Jesus's standards. His fault is not laziness, but the fact that he does not trust his master. He did not make what was entrusted to him by his master into his own cause. He did not take any risks.

What is Jesus saying to us with this parable? I think the answer to this question is not difficult. The parable tells us something essential about the relationship between God and us human beings. God is the one who gives us our talents. We have not given life to ourselves: it is a gift of God entrusted to us, a talent for which we, God's own image, have been given responsibility.

Life is thus both a gift and a task. Human beings have the task of making something of the lives we have been given by God, of unfolding the possibilities that lie in the world.

The parable is admonishing us as human beings to be ready to dare new things, to take on risks. We human beings have had life breathed into us through the love of the Creator, the one who also makes us creative and imaginative. For God, creation is not completed. In a certain sense, it is to be taken further each day, not least through our own human initiative.

Not all human beings have the same responsibilities. In the parable, Jesus distinguished between persons who have been given much and others to whom less has been given. What is decisive is not how many talents one has, but that one makes the best of whatever natural and supernatural gifts one has. God demands from us only what we possess.

Upon his return, the master asks accountability from his servants. They are to give an accounting of their stewardship. So, we are not autocratic "makers." We are only stewards of goods that ultimately do not belong to us, goods that we have received and must return in the end. In any case, we cannot ultimately possess anything in this world.

Indeed, this parable only appears to be about money and inanimate things. What God entrusts to us is something living: our natural and supernatural strengths and abilities, and indeed the gift of life itself. Every living thing wants to grow and mature; it "puts itself in play" and risks something. The parable of the talents asks that we dare to become truly living persons, which means setting ourselves to work for a truly human culture in which there is room for everyone.

It gives us the perspective of hope that can mobilize our responsibility. God entrusts much into our hands, into our self-reliance and autonomy. What is asked of us is to trust in life and to have the courage to really live. We can take the risk of living, for God has risked life with us.

Chapter Four

THE WAY OF THE CROSS
(Reflections for Lent, Holy Thursday, and Good Friday)

Ash Wednesday
(Reflection for Ash Wednesday)

To encounter oneself on Ash Wednesday is to meet oneself at a difficult intersection of life. The day before, *Mardi Gras*, had been a time for masquerades, for foolishness, for dancing and laughter, for a more or less cultivated playfulness—whether as a day of joy or of just fleeing into pleasure without judgment from the outside world.

But Ash Wednesday takes off the masks. It does not intend to take the joy of life away from us. It does not ask us to walk around with a scowl. But Ash Wednesday does put the reality and truth of our existence before our eyes, unvarnished, without further ado. It reminds us of our creatureliness, our fragility, our transience: "You are dust, and to dust you shall return" (Gen 3:19). Ash Wednesday locates our life. It admonishes us not to forget that we are embraced by death in the middle of life, that we do not possess our own life, that our need to give our life away (whether we want to or not) is dead certain, that not even for a moment are we capable of living by our own power.

In all of this, however, Ash Wednesday also shows us the gift that our life is. It says to us, With every breath, you receive life anew; you receive life from the hand of your Creator who breathes his breath of life into you in every moment of your existence and who wants you to have life and have it in abundance.

The biblical Creation account expresses this message with a deeply revealing image: like a potter, God forms the human being from clay and blows his own breath into him. That means that as human beings we are fragile clay. But as human beings we are also given form as an expression of the Creator, his image and likeness. The breath of God breathes in us. We are life from God's life and share in his creativity, his inventiveness.

So, this day and its message tell us of both our greatness and our poverty, of both the grandeur and the fragility of our existence, our life and our death. To encounter oneself on Ash Wednesday means meeting oneself in the great tensions of our existence—in the tensions between creative power and a givenness over which we are powerless, between freedom and inexorableness, between infinity and finitude, between life and death.

The message of Ash Wednesday can be summed up in a few words from Blaise Pascal's *Pensées* (par. 526): "The knowledge of God without that of man's misery causes pride. The knowledge of man's misery without that of God causes despair. The knowledge of Jesus Christ constitutes the middle course, because in Him we find both God and our misery."[1]

This message of Ash Wednesday found its unique and unsurpassable fulfillment in Jesus Christ. In Jesus Christ,

God has become involved—completely and without reservation—with us human beings; in him, God has taken our limitation, our frailty, and our death upon himself. God "emptied himself, taking the form of a slave, being born in human likeness. And being found in human form, he humbled himself and became obedient to the point of death—even death on a cross" (Phil 2:7–8).

Even the act of creation, by which God creates us from nothing and makes us his counterparts and calls us into communion with him, finds its unsurpassable intensification in the incarnation: in the incarnation, God not only creates us human beings in his image but makes himself our image for what it means to be human. Even more than this, God shows us his greatness in lowliness: "He had no form or majesty that we should look at him, nothing in his appearance that we should desire him. He was despised and rejected by others; a man of suffering and acquainted with infirmity"—so it says in the Servant Songs in Isaiah (Isa 53:2–3).

In a singular way, Jesus Christ is the image of God and the image of the true human being. He shows us that it is not only in our grandeur and our reaching for the stars that we are the image of God. But, also and precisely in our limitation, vulnerability, and fragility; in our failure, too, we breathe the breath of God, and God is close to us.

And so, we must not close our eyes to the limitations of our existence and to our shadow. On the contrary: when we become clear about our situation, when we shed light upon and illuminate our existence with the light of faith, then for the first time will we find a direction; only then will we grab hold of our chance for real freedom.

LONGING FOR LOVE (THIRD SUNDAY OF LENT, YEAR A: JOHN 4:1–42)

Let us reflect on the encounter between Jesus and the woman at the well, in order to discover what the story can tell us about our own lives and what it might mean for our faith.

The human traits of Jesus are what initially strike us in his encounter with the woman of Samaria. A thirsty man comes to a well. He is tired from his journeys, thirsty from the dust of the roads. In the midday heat, he asks for a mouthful of water. He asks the woman who herself had come to draw water to help him obtain some of this refreshing water.

With this request made to a Samaritan woman—which for Jesus as a Jewish man was downright scandalous—Jesus touches on an old conflict between Jews and Samaritans. He is confronted with the centuries-old stalemates, disagreements, and mutual exclusions between the ancient northern kingdom of Samaria and the temple religion of Judea. Hostility and intrigues have ripped apart the people of the Old Covenant. But Jesus will not be defined by the old barriers of national and religious identity, and thus does not deny his own human need for this thirst-quenching water.

Then Jesus shifts the conversation to the real issue facing the woman. It is about her inner thirst to speak truly, about her need for love and security, for a partner who satisfies all longing for love—for someone with whom one can be completely at home. But no relationship she has entered into has quenched her thirst. Jesus makes no accusations against her on this account. He simply confirms that she has told the truth in saying she does not have a husband, someone who loves her in the way she longs in her heart to be loved. He knows her individual truth: She has searched and searched again, over and over, was disappointed each time, and then again went out searching. She feels her own limits, is perhaps even suffering under the weight of her immoderate longing for happiness, from her permanent self-preoccupation that has not gotten her what she most wants.

In conversing with Jesus, she begins to see that he has something for her, that he has something to give her. She begins to realize how great the thirst for love and security is that has settled over her life like a shadow; and she begins to sense that, in the presence of Jesus, she can accept this shadow and be reconciled with it.

Jesus broadens the horizon of the woman at the well to include God, when previously her vision had circled endlessly around herself. She increasingly discovers in Jesus the well she has sought throughout her life. And so she asks him, whom through knowledge of the heart she sees to be a prophet, about true worship.

It is in worship that our longing for a home, for security, and for love is fulfilled. When I fall down on my knees and worship God as God, I free myself from the need to draw everything to myself, to ask again and again what is in it for me. It is then that I can forget myself. For God has touched me and taken me into his own heart. Then I, already embraced, am truly and completely at home.

This conversation has so affected the woman that she begins to believe: "Can he be the Messiah?" she asks herself (see John 4:29). She leaves her water jar behind at the well; what previously had seemed so important has lost its importance. She "must" share what she has received; it almost compels her onward. She becomes a messenger of the gospel, and many Samaritans become believers in Jesus because of the woman's testimony.

An Encounter at the Well of Life (Third Sunday of Lent, Year A: John 4:1–42)

The gospel story of the Samaritan woman at Jacob's well seeks to awaken courage. It says to us that the thirst for true life and thus for God is alive in our day, much more alive than most of us suspect.

The Gospel begins with a natural request for water, an everyday request. But it is soon clear that there is something more behind this request. For Middle Eastern people, water is a symbol of the fulfillment of our thirst for life. Yet, life has more than a biological dimension; it is more than mere survival. We are able to live in a truly human way only when there is light and meaning in our lives. We are able to live in a human way only when we are accepted by others and can use our life to benefit others. Life and love are deeply related.

But we must often dig out our blocked well of life and love. We human beings, who are always searching for God, are also seeking out other human beings who can help us live and open up to us the meaning of life. "I have no one," laments the sick man in John's Gospel (John 5:7). This lament is also the urgent cry of many contemporary people. Perhaps loneliness and alienation have never been greater than they are in our present mass society.

The Gospel speaks of our need for human encounters and the blessing they are for us. On the face of it, this Samaritan woman has had many encounters. But they all went wrong. She has had five husbands, and the one she currently has is not a husband to her. It is a failed existence.

It is only in her encounter with Jesus that the well of life is opened up to her. Jesus, as this Gospel points out, is the one who opens himself completely to others. He does so without prejudice and reservation. His disciples are astounded and appalled that he is conversing with a woman, with a foreign Samaritan woman, and particularly with a woman like this. But how does he do it?

Jesus gets to the bottom of the questions and challenges of this woman, and he opens up new possibilities of life for her. He is both the messenger and the bringer of new life, the gift and the giver. So, Jesus can say of himself, "I am."[2] Jesus himself is the place of encountering and honoring God; he is the Messiah, he alone! He is the Savior of the world (John 4:42). Our task is to go to him as the well of life and to lead others to him. We too must keep digging at the well, as the believers of the first covenant dug at and named Jacob's well; we must keep digging at the well that the church has also been working at since the days of the apostles and of the great church fathers of East and West; we must keep digging at the well to which saints, known and unknown, have ever since come to drink and encounter Christ.

The fruitfulness of our work stands and falls on our bringing ourselves again and again to a personal encounter with Christ: in prayer, in meditation, and in the sacraments.

We can be messengers of life only if the one who is life can be seen in us, when we let him work in us. In the end, the baptismal font is the well of life. The waters of new life flow here. And we receive the bread of life in the Eucharist. This scene at the well of Jacob repeats itself every time we gather at the baptismal font, and it reaches its deepest fulfillment in the Eucharist.

We should celebrate the liturgy in such a way that our human soul, so often exhausted, can rest and breathe, that a space of silence can arise in which personal encounter with Christ becomes possible, and in which we can taste something of eternal life, eternal peace, and eternal joy.

To Be Able to Wait (Third Sunday of Lent, Year C: Luke 13:1–9)

"Lord, let this tree alone for one more year, while I dig around it and put manure on it. Perhaps it will bear fruit next year" (see Luke 13:8–9). These words reflect the experience of a farmer who knows that one cannot force anything out of nature, that instead one must have staying power. As humans, we can only dig, plant, fertilize, and water; we cannot "make" anything grow.

With this parable from the realm of nature Jesus is telling us about the pedagogy of God. It is a basic motif of the Bible that God has infinite patience with his rebellious people and with all of us. Truly there would be enough reasons for God to strike back. Jewish philosopher Martin Buber (1878–1965) said, "Success is not one of the names of God." God leaves time for growth, and God gives us time. The church fathers often thought about and pointed to this pedagogy of God, about how God walks with his people step by step in history, often using very small steps in order to get to the goal.

This "law of steps" applies not only to the large picture of salvation history, but also to each small individual faith story. It is consistent with human pedagogy and even more with that of God: we are to accompany young people with a lot of patience on their respective very personal journeys of faith. We can only lend assistance; we cannot make faith itself happen. Another must be the source of growth. Faith remains a gift of the gratuitous grace of God, the fruit of each individual's free choice.

We must always take a new chance with the young people entrusted to us, as God has done with us. Resignation is not at all called for. That would mean giving up. It would not only mean giving up on faith in God and in God's possibilities of raising up children of Abraham from stones, that is, on God's ability to raise up children of faith. We would also be giving up our faith in the young people who have been entrusted to us. Just as God does not give up on us but appeals to us again and again and even outright runs after us, so we must not give up on anyone.

When Jesus speaks of the vineyard and the fig tree, he is using common biblical images for the chosen people. We are the vineyard and the fig tree, we the church. Planting the vineyard and caring for the fig tree means building up the church.

Already in the third century, church writer Tertullian (160–220) put it this way: "One Christian is no Christian." Rootedness in a church community is important in a world that has become anonymous. But what is essential is that we leave space for the work of God. We are not to give up, but are to say with the worker in the vineyard, "Perhaps he or she will still bear fruit."

A HEART THAT SEES (FOURTH SUNDAY OF LENT, YEAR A: JOHN 9:1–41)

All the miracles of Jesus reported in the Gospel of John are called "signs" (Greek *semeia*), and are deliberately named so by John.[3] These Johannine signs function in the way that symbols from our everyday life function. For example, if a man gives a red rose to a woman, on the surface it is just a flower he is giving. But more deeply, and in truth, this gift means much more and we all understand that immediately.

The healing of the man born blind (see John 9:1–41) is the fifth of the signs of Jesus in John's Gospel. First of all, there is the event itself: a man blind from birth is healed by Jesus so that he can now see. Jesus does not make this happen with a verbal command, for instance by saying, "I decree it, receive your sight!" Instead he heals the blind man with an action; he mixes saliva and earth into a paste, spreads it on the sick eyes and tells the man born blind to go and wash in the pool of Siloam. The man's full healing takes place through a holistic, very human process; the blind man experiences it through his own senses and himself has a role in the process. So far, this is an observable, factual event.

In truth, though, there is a deeper reality at work. This is clearly evident in the discussion among the Pharisees, the parents of the blind man, and the man himself that follows the healing: the parties are arguing over the question of who this Jesus is. The Pharisees remain in blindness, stubbornness, and unbelief, while the man born blind who now sees slowly finds his way to faith. He advances step by step all the way to the highest christological confession. First, in the argument with the Pharisees, he confesses, "He is a prophet." In the end, he responds to the question of Jesus ("Do you believe in the Song of Man?") with a confession of faith: "Lord, I believe." In the Book of Daniel, the Son of Man is a heavenly figure who is led to stand before God. This is said of him: "To him was given dominion and glory and kingship, that all peoples, nations, and languages should serve him. His dominion is an everlasting dominion that shall not pass away, and his kingship is one that shall never be destroyed" (Dan 7:14). The man born blind who now sees understands something of the mystery of the person of Jesus: he has come forth from God, and great power and dominion over the world is entrusted to him. And so it makes complete sense that the man born blind who now sees should bow down before Jesus as a sign of gratitude, even worship.

Thus, the meaning of the "sign" of the blind man's healing becomes clear: Jesus heals the blindness of hearts, the darkness of unbelief. He makes the blind man's heart a seeing heart, and the man can now believe. The healing of the blind eyes of this man becomes a sign for the healing of the whole human being, opening him to God in order to let the light of faith illuminate his life. This also explains the meaning of Jesus's testimony before he heals the blind man: "As long as I am in the world, I am the light of the world" (John 9:5).

NEIGHBOR LOVE (HOLY THURSDAY, MASS OF THE LORD'S SUPPER: JOHN 13:1–5)

In a gesture whose symbolic power cannot be overstated, Jesus, on the eve of his death, summarizes one more time the meaning and significance of his message and of his whole life. He kneels to do what in his day was the lowest and most scorned task of a slave: he washes his disciples' feet and in so doing expresses drastically and plainly that he has not come to be served, but to serve and to give his life for all.

Once more, he reminds his disciples of the past: of the way in which he accepted as his friends the sick, the poor, and the weak, all of those who existed at the margins of society. He calls to mind the parable of the Good Samaritan, who selflessly serves someone who had fallen into the hands of robbers. He demonstrates once again that he had always behaved like a servant among his disciples.

The foot washing on the evening before his suffering and death is, as it were, a summary of the whole life and ministry of Jesus. It sums up what he has been doing and what the life of Christians is about. "For I have set you an example, that you also should do as I have done to you" (John 13:15).

Thank God, there have been Christians, women and men, in every age who have allowed themselves to be so deeply affected by Jesus as to devote themselves to service of the poor and orphans, the sick and dying, to children as well as the aged, to prisoners and refugees.

As the friend of human beings, the God of Jesus wants to meet and help human beings who are in need and in distress through the care of other human beings. That such human beings, women and men, exist in such large numbers also in our day; that God awakens, empowers, and encourages such people—for all this we want and ought, first of all, to give God thanks.

It is only when there is a certain "spiritual groundwater level" that we can live with more humanity and tolerance, more respect for life, more dignity for the dying—but also more respect for those who are different, for strangers, for those released from prison, for those who have failed many times in life, for those who have slipped morally. Such love, such *caritas*, incites us to a hope that does not end but begins to shine precisely at the limits of our human possibilities.

The Opened Heart (Good Friday, The Passion of the Lord: John 18:1—19:42)

"One of the soldiers pierced his side with a spear, and at once blood and water came out" (John 19:34). Such an act of cruelty at the end point of this story can only be heard with consternation. One who spent his life doing good deeds for the poor, the marginalized, and for sinners; one who proclaimed and lived the mercy of God—still he was imprisoned, handed over to the contemptuous mob, condemned while innocent, brutally tortured, beaten, despised, his hands and feet drilled through with nails, and hung for three long hours on the gallows of the cross. The thrust of a spear into a heart stilled by death seems to be the end point of the story.

This end point, however, is also the climax of the story. This opened heart allows us to see into his heart, and so reveals to us the heart of the Father. For whoever sees Jesus sees the Father (John 14:9). And so the opened heart of Jesus reveals to us the heart of God, whose heart beats with love and mercy; God, whose heart is pierced, wounded, and broken by human heartlessness; God, whose heart remains wide open to all our human need and suffering. The heart of Jesus reveals to us God as the Father of mercies (2 Cor 1:3), as the one who is rich in mercy (Eph 2:4).

Already in the covenant with Moses, God could not overlook the plight of his people (Exod 3:7–8, 16–17). "The LORD, a God merciful and gracious, slow to anger, and abounding in steadfast love and faithfulness": in just this way, the people of the Old Covenant summarize their experience of God after having been freed from Egypt (Exod 34:6). Jesus fully proclaims God as the merciful Father who takes the prodigal son into his arms with compassion and mercy, accepting him and restoring to him all the privileges of God's people (Luke 15:20).

But even that is not enough. It is only the pierced heart of Jesus on the cross that allows us to gaze into all the depths of the love and the mercy of the Father. In Jesus, God did not want to give us a high priest who could not identify with our human suffering and weakness and need (Heb 4:15). So much did God love the world that he gave his only Son (John 3:16). He emptied himself and turned toward us; he humbled himself and became obedient to the point of death, even death on a cross (Phil 2:8).

Even God could go no further than this. Even God could do no more than this. We could not even think of or hope for more than this. The cross is the focal point and the high point of the revelation of God, of the revelation of God's love and mercy.

The opened heart of Jesus on the cross lets us peer into the center of the heart of the Father. "The cross is the most profound condescension of God to human beings and to what we—especially in difficult and painful moments—look on as our unhappy destiny. The cross is like a touch of eternal love upon the most painful wounds of our earthly existence" (John Paul II, *Dives in Misericordia* 8).[4]

All dreams of the progress of humankind, all hopes for peace on earth eventually come to naught. The heartlessness of the world is clear. All the misery and torture, all the injustice and hatred in the world, all that is unredeemed and in need of salvation in humanity becomes clear. The hardened hearts of human beings are laid bare. These are the spears thrust into the heart of our civilization, the spears thrust into the heart of our hearts, the spears thrust into the heart of Jesus, for those who are so inhumanly treated are Jesus's brothers and sisters, and our brothers and sisters; they are like children of the Father in heaven.

All this, then, must also go through our heart like a spear. How far have we let that happen? When will we awaken? When will we finally allow ourselves to be seized by the mercy of God? When will we open our hearts to a new civilization of love and mercy? The opened heart of Jesus is a question put to our own hearts. It is an appeal to all of us, each in our own circumstances, to work together for a world in which it is not self-interest that counts, but where solidarity, compassion, and mercy are the true measure of human culture.

"BY HIS BRUISES WE ARE HEALED" (GOOD FRIDAY, THE PASSION OF THE LORD: ISAIAH 52:13—53:12)

We want to look upon the crucified one to let ourselves be stirred by him and to enter into the mystery of his passion.

Let us look once again at his body covered with lacerations and wounds, at his distorted limbs, at the wounds in his outstretched hands and feet, at the wound in his side reaching to his heart, at the cruel crown of thorns surrounding his head, at his face grown pale, at his dying eyes. Brutal violence is at work here. Blind hatred strikes out against Jesus. He was unjustly accused, condemned in a trial that mocked all justice, cruelly flogged, scoffed at, ridiculed, and despised. The last remnant of his dignity was taken from him. He died the most shameful death that the world of his time could contemplate. "A man of suffering and acquainted with infirmity" (Isa 53:3).

So, Jesus hangs on the cross representing all who have been crucified in the long history of humankind—even in our day. After the destruction of Jerusalem, there was not enough wood for all whom the Romans wanted to punish by crucifixion at the city walls.

And there are many among us here and now who have their crosses to carry, their illnesses to bear, day in and out their sufferings to withstand or their disabilities to cope with. There is so much suffering and poverty in our world. Our modern civilization is filled with forces and structures that make persons physically and spiritually sick.

I am not referring only to bodily deprivations, illnesses, suffering, and wounds. They are awful enough. But I am also thinking of the spiritual wounds, the inner illnesses, injuries, belittlements and humiliations, slander, and discrimination that many people have to endure. I am thinking of the bodily and spiritual violations committed against children and that so deeply harm them.

Truly, one despairs in the face of so much suffering. One despairs of a world in which all of this happens every single day. In fact, we would need to despair if we were not able to say on Good Friday, "Surely he has borne our infirmities and carried our diseases….By his bruises we are healed" (see Isa 53:4–5).

The Way of the Cross

We can only imagine what Jesus experienced in those three bitter hours on the cross: embitterment and disappointment in the face of so much treachery, vulgarity, mendacity, and wickedness; but even more of his will to forgive and pardon, of his love for us and dedication to the will of the Father. One of the thieves expressed it clearly: "We indeed have been condemned justly, for we are getting what we deserve for our deeds, but this man has done nothing wrong" (Luke 23:41).

He could not simply look down at all the pain of the world, the pain of human beings, whom he created in his image and likeness, from the glory of heaven. It moved him to mercy. In the freedom of love, he wanted to be with us and for us, to be like us in all things but sin. So, he put up no resistance, not striking back, but surrendered himself willingly into the hands of human beings. Thus, he broke open the vicious circle of evil and violence and counterviolence. In Jesus, the powers of deception, hatred, and violence have exhausted themselves; they have come to their death. The logic of his love has conquered the logic of hatred. Forgiveness and reconciliation are the deepest reality and have come into the world as new possibilities. "By his bruises we are healed" (Isa 53:5; see also 1 Pet 2:24).

This is the hope that we Christians should pass on to others. That is our mission. We have often neglected and forgotten the healing mission he gave to his disciples and that he himself accomplished for us on the cross. Salvation and healing belong together. As disciples of Jesus, we Christians should be people who open ourselves to the sorrows of others; we are not to look away from them, but to notice and listen to them; we are to be people who help carry the burdens of others, who suffer with them and are merciful to them. Rightly, we are hearing more often of a more holistic pastoral care; it is needed in our time. We need a new culture of mercy. Only in the power of the cross can we be reconciled and create a new common future.

THE NAKED TRUTH (REFLECTION FOR GOOD FRIDAY)

"They divided his clothes among themselves by casting lots" (Matt 27:35). We learn this from the passion narratives. Good Friday is the hour of naked truth, not in an abstract sense but bodily and in person. Jesus stands there: naked, with nothing at all, exposed to every shameless look, given over to mockery, surrendered to raw and brutal violence. He stands for us: completely naked, without clothes, without reputation, and without dignity, surrendered to his tormentors, slandered, brutally tortured and tormented, abandoned by all, quite solitary, all alone. "O bleeding head, so wounded, reviled and put to scorn!" *Ecce homo:* "Behold, the human being" (see John 19:5).

In his nakedness, Jesus is the naked truth about us human beings. This "behold the human being" is true also of us. Naked we come into the world, and naked we leave it. In between the two, however, we must reckon with everything that might happen. Not just beautiful clothes and some jewelry. Even then, we are all more or less afflicted. We may seek to surround ourselves with prosperity, with respect, with influence, with relationships. We may want to be presentable. We may prefer to put on a mask and make ourselves something in front of others. Only with great difficulty can we bear the naked truth about ourselves.

Our world has its sorrow and its shame. We rush from action to action, from one experience to the next. We build up gigantic worlds of technology and pleasure. What do we not think of to divert and distract ourselves, and to make everything seem fine? Continually we turn away from ourselves and from the truth about us; we flee from ourselves.

Yet at some point everyone enters into the school of suffering. At some point everyone meets their limits. At some point we are confronted with the naked truth. And so, the suffering unhappily appears: in unexpected misfortune, in a serious illness, in the breakdown of a relationship, in failure, loneliness, unjust treatment and suspicion, in the experience of failure and futility.

Our shadow and the shadows of our lives always accompany us; no one can jump over their own shadow. And, obviously, no one can escape death.

Usually we hide the suffering, consider it an accident to be fixed. Many use alcohol or drugs to try to find the way. And if not those, we have devised many methods and means to push away suffering and pain, both physical and mental, and thus end up with the substitute suffering of neuroses.

Only truth will set us free. Good Friday teaches us to look naked truth in the eye. "Behold the human being": yes, we are this way; we are this human being.

Jesus shows us the naked truth about ourselves, but even more he shows us the naked truth about God. In Jesus's being stripped, God too has let himself be stripped. God has given up all God's power, strength, and glory. God emptied and handed himself over, became poor, powerless, and naked. God did not and does not want to leave us alone with the naked truth about ourselves, for without God we are not able to endure it. God places God's own dignity at risk, in order to save our dignity. God does not want us to be alone. God wants to share our suffering, pain, abandonment, defamation, fear, and even the night of our death with us. The cross reveals to us the unreservedly naked love of God.

It is only because, standing before us naked and bare, Jesus reveals the naked love of God to us that he can also give us the power and courage not to hide from ourselves and from others, not to run away from the truth of our lives, but to stand before it, to accept it, and in great patience, to bear it. Without God and the cross there are only two possibilities: revolt or resignation. It is only in the school of suffering of the cross that the truth about ourselves becomes bearable. Only before the cross can we learn again to deal with our weakness, our suffering, our fear, and our disappointments. It is precisely in our nakedness that we can encounter God's naked love, discover God's light in the middle of our night, and in the middle of our own coldness experience the warmth of his all-healing and transforming love.

Indeed, just as Jesus stands naked before us, just as he hangs on the cross, just so does the truth become clear to us: God does not take suffering away from us; God does not wipe away our problems; God does not give us some cheap, easy answer. God's answer is to accompany us and so give us the strength to do as he does: to share both the sufferings and joys of others. Because God has brought the naked truth of God's love into the naked truth of our life, we need no longer be crushed by suffering; instead, we can break open to a love that heals and transforms us. We can become companions for other human beings who are lost in the night or who find themselves on a tightrope between bitterness and resignation.

The Cross (Reflection for Good Friday)

When we look at the cross, we see Jesus's whip marks from being flogged, his muscles stretched tight, his blood-covered head, and his face grown pale in death, the open wound at his side, and his open heart from which blood and water flow. We see the cold-blooded cruelty of his Roman executioners, hear the sarcastic words of his enemies, and know the cowardice and betrayal of his disciples. We see that Jesus is terribly alone and abandoned in this hour. But we also see his arms spread wide—opened wide in order to embrace each and every one of us, even in the midst of the indifference and hatred, the pain and suffering.

When we look at the cross, we see how great, how immeasurably great is God's love for us human beings, for every single one of us. For our sake, for our salvation, God underwent all of this. "I have done this for you," says the Lord; then he asks us: What will you do for me? What have you done to me? How have you responded to my love? "My burden in thy passion, Lord, thou hast borne for me. For it was my transgression, which brought this woe to thee."[5]

"They look on the one whom they have pierced" (Zech 12:10). These words from the prophet appear a second time in Sacred Scripture. In the final book of the New Testament, the visionary of Patmos writes to the seven churches of Asia Minor. He greets them in Jesus Christ and then says that Jesus "loves us and freed us from our sins by his blood, and made us to be a kingdom, priests serving his God and Father." And then he adds, "Look! He is coming with the clouds; every eye will see him, even those who pierced him" (Rev 1:5–7).

The crucified is not the wretched one who has perished; he is the one who is coming, the "Alpha and the Omega." He is the one "who is and who was and who is to come" (Rev 1:8). He is the "judge of the living and the dead" (Acts 10:42). The cross at which we gaze is our measure, our orientation marker, our guide. It is the axis on which the world turns, on which our life hangs and must be aligned, but also the foundation on which our life may always begin again.

Many today would prefer not to look at the cross. We do not want to endure the sight of it. We think it ought to be taken down and removed. But do we know what happens when we take down and remove the cross, when we set it aside?

The cross is a symbol of solidarity with and mercy for all who carry crosses in this world, the poor, the sick, those who are disabled or who suffer, the persecuted and outcast, the grieving and the anxious, the dying. The cross is a sign of love and mercy, a sign of nonviolence, of willingness to serve and to reconcile. To look on the crucified one means measuring our lives by these values and making them the measure of all our dealings.

If we can no longer endure the sight of the cross and if we wish to set aside the values for which the cross stands, then it will always be Good Friday in this world of ours. Then there will no longer be the Easter light of hope for a more human world. But whenever one looks upon the cross and the crucified one, whenever one orients oneself on the cross, there and then does the cross become a sign of hope, a sign of a new culture of life, of humanity, and of mercy.

THE HEART OF JESUS (REFLECTION FOR GOOD FRIDAY)

The Feast of the Sacred Heart of Jesus is one of the newest feast days to be added to the church liturgical calendar (in 1856).[6] And veneration of the Sacred Heart, as the practice is known to us, originated only in the modern era. But its core idea reaches back to the basic message of the Bible.

Many Christians think that in the Old Testament God is revealed only as a judging and punishing God before whom we should tremble in fear. But the prophet Ezekiel depicts God as having a heart for his people; Ezekiel says that God cares for God's people in the way a shepherd cares for his sheep (Ezek 34:11–16).

And when we hear in the New Testament about how Jesus lived and acted, about the way in which he encountered people, we recognize in him the good shepherd described by Ezekiel: Jesus searches out the lost sheep; he seeks out people wherever they have fallen, whether from their own mistakes or through an unavoidable fate. He seeks them out in their isolation and lack of perspective. Jesus's message of the saving love of God becomes concrete in the way he turns toward people at the margins of society in his time. He searches them out in order to give them what they had lost or had never been given in the first place: trust and love. He gives them communion with the God who has a heart for human beings, the God who heals all our wounds and injuries with his infinite love.

Just how serious God is about love becomes most clear in the suffering and death of his Son on the cross. In the cross of Jesus, the meaning of this boundless love of God becomes clear in an equally drastic way: it is ready to go to extreme limits—even to the extent of allowing itself to be broken for the sake of the beloved ones. This love does not only give us some sort of gift; it gives itself to us. "No one has greater love than this, to lay down one's life for one's friends" (John 15:13). In the pierced heart of Jesus, we are able to look into God's own heart. It is the clearest, most unmistakable sign of God's boundless love. On the cross, it becomes clear: "God is love" (1 John 4:8, 16). Only such a love could really save us. For this love does not come down from above or from the outside in; rather, for our sake it is ready to arise entirely, completely from below, from the inside, from the heart, to heal all of the world's hatred and injustice. Jesus took our burden and our guilt completely onto himself, so that we could be saved and thus freed to live from this same love ourselves.

The pierced heart of Jesus can open our eyes to what is most important in our own lives. In the end, only one thing matters: love. This is the greatest command of Jesus. It is the fulfillment of the entire law.

The first response to the love of God made clear in the pierced heart of Jesus can only be gratitude. We are to be grateful to have such a Shepherd and Savior who leads and loves us and to whom we can entrust ourselves completely. Let us not lose the joy of being Christians. To be a Christian is not a burden but a liberation. To be a Christian means to know and thus to live from the knowledge that we are loved and ultimately have nothing to fear—nothing at all from other human beings and even less from God. Why, then, are we so forgetful and lacking in gratitude?

Devotion to the pierced heart of Jesus can open our eyes to the truth that our Christian lives can succeed only if we adopt the fundamental attitude of Jesus himself, that is, if our love, grounded in our relationship with God, can grow to include other human beings, whom we recognize as our sisters and brothers. It is only when we, too, have a heart for other human beings that we are truly Christian. It is only when we do not close ourselves off from others and their needs, only when we go out to them, forgiving, comforting, strengthening, helping, and supporting them. We, too, should be good shepherds, good companions for our fellow human beings. Just as God ceaselessly speaks an unconditional yes to us, so we must speak the same yes to others.

What is at the core of a credible Christian life is that we not encounter our fellow human beings from a distance, meeting them self-righteously from above, but that we encounter them fully aware of our own brokenness. We, too, carry around with us wounds and injuries that can only be healed through the saving love of God. They will be redeemed by the one who in his love allowed himself to be wounded, so that our wounds might be healed: "By his wounds you have been healed" (1 Pet 2:24).

Redeemed through the Blood of Christ (Reflection for Good Friday)

In one sentence, Jesus summarizes the entirety of his message: "This is my blood of the covenant, which is poured out for many" (Mark 14:24).[7]

In a new way, Jesus revealed the God who is with and for us, who never abandons us but leads and accompanies us along our entire life path. He even goes beyond the Old Testament in this regard. For, in Jesus Christ, God himself became human, completely one of us, like us in all things but sin. God has entered entirely into the heights and depths of our lives, into the joys and sufferings of human existence. In him, God suffered hunger and thirst, took our sufferings upon himself, and died a miserable death on the cross. Through the painful death of Jesus on the cross, God showed us that God loves us literally to death, and that God has given himself wholly and completely for us and for all. Through the blood of Jesus shed on the cross, God's covenant with us has been sealed forever and God's limitless love for all has been definitively revealed.

God is not some remote being; God is our God, the God who has come completely close to us in Jesus Christ and who has sealed an eternal covenant with us in Jesus's blood shed on the cross.

"Redeemed through the blood of Christ" means we can now live as redeemed human beings: we are redeemed from fear, for we have been saved by God's love; redeemed from fixation on accomplishment and success; redeemed from the enslaving compulsion to have and then to have more; redeemed from the suspicion that in the end everything is meaningless and in vain; redeemed from the sadness and miserliness that so many succumb to, and from the egoism and individualism that hordes and can let go of nothing. We are able to live in a different way: we have been redeemed through the blood of

Christ; we have been saved and are now held in God's love. God has sealed an eternal covenant with us. God is our God, and we are God's people. And so, we can be filled with joy and celebration.

Is this not a joyful and liberating message that is proclaimed to us in every celebration of the Eucharist? It is a message that can sustain our lives and fill them with meaning; it is a message that gives us strength, joy, and hope—which we need to live now and into the future, even in the face of our death. This is a faith of which we need not at all be ashamed, but that we can confess freely and joyfully.

This is a message that deserves to be passed on. This faith is the most worthwhile of all things. But we are only able to pass on in a vital and convincing way what we ourselves have lived, what is inwardly convincing to us. And so, we must allow faith to say something new to us ourselves; we must allow the love, mercy, and salvation of our God to enter completely into us; we must allow them to grow warmer and then burst into flame in our own hearts and lives, if we want to set them alight in others. We must ourselves become convinced Christians if we want this faith to have a convincing effect on others.

We must turn back and repent, bringing ourselves again before the God who has saved us through the precious blood of Jesus. Only in him will we find life and salvation. We must again become aware of what gives a foundation and content to our lives; we must allow ourselves to be overtaken again by God's love. We must not allow ourselves to be ungrateful for God's loving us literally to death or to leave that love unanswered. We must become more prayerful human beings, more prayerful families, more prayerful communities, and more prayerful churches. We must once again take part, more regularly and more thoroughly, in the celebration of the Eucharist, in which God's unending love and mercy become concretely present to us.

The message of our being redeemed through the blood of Jesus Christ was and remains the deepest foundation of the idea of the inherent dignity of every human being and for the desire for peace among peoples. And so we Christians have the right and duty to raise our voices in the face of the increasing dechristianization of public life.

Redeemed by the blood of Christ is a message and a reality relevant not only to past centuries; it is a message that we need, and one that has the ability to help shape a more human future.

The Cross: Victory of Truth (Reflection for Good Friday)

In a concentration camp, a Jewish boy shared a few pages of Holy Scripture with another Jewish sufferer. This was strictly forbidden and was considered a conspiracy with the aim of rebellion. The young man was not only ruthlessly beaten and flogged by the SS henchmen before the assembly of the camp, but was hung on the gallows for all to see. One of the prisoners who were forced to stand and watch this exclaimed loudly, "Where is God? Where has God gone?" A deep and tense silence followed. Then someone else lifted his hand, pointed to the one who had been hanged, and cried out, "There's where God is!"[8]

As a Jewish believer living fully in the spirit of the Old Testament, this prisoner knew that God is with the suffering, the slain, the condemned, and the damned of this earth. God identifies with them and suffers with them. As Christians, shouldn't we know this even more deeply? For, in Jesus Christ, God himself has descended to share our human life, descended as far as the gallows of the cross. God has identified with every single one of us and has allied himself with us. God joins us on the way of suffering; God drinks the bitter cup of death with us.

Thanks be to God, the terrible time of the Third Reich, when concentration camps spewed smoke from their crematoria, has long past. We live in a free society that is committed to human rights. Nonetheless, the history of suffering among human beings continues in our day. Every single day, we hear of how millions of human beings suffer from hunger, so many of them dying. Time and again, we hear reports of unimaginable horror, torture, and cruelty. We all know stories of people dying tragically, of people suffering from incurable diseases. We have our own share of violence, lies, and meanness, of murderous stares and wounding words. Many are overwhelmed and discouraged, or stand alone and lonely.

The cross is not only the truth about human beings; it is also the truth about God. It points out to us that God is not some unmoved mover, enthroned above the clouds; God is a God of human beings. It is especially the poor, the weak, and the suffering to whom God is close; God loves such people most of all. In Jesus Christ, God has taken on all the suffering and guilt of the world—doing so freely, motivated only by grace and mercy: all the meanness, lies, treachery, injustice, and pain. God has been spared nothing, so close to us has God chosen to be. Thus, there is no situation that is completely cut off from God, completely godless. God has become like us in all things, except sin.

The cross is the victory of truth over lies, of love over hatred, of life over death. We are united not only with the crucified, but also with the resurrected Christ. For us, Jesus Christ is the basis and the beginning of new life. He gives us new courage to live, a whole new vision of hope.

IN THE CROSS IS SALVATION (REFLECTION FOR GOOD FRIDAY)

The cross does not prettify or cover over anything whatsoever. Rather, the cross reveals the truth about us human beings and our sins. It says to us, yes, we are this way; this is what we do to one another; that is how we operate. The cross is the unvarnished truth, and it is only the truth that can set us free.

The cross makes it possible for us to acknowledge the difficult truth. For the cross, which is the truth about our human guilt and sin, is also the truth about the far greater mercy of God and of the forgiving and reconciling love of God. In the cross, God intended and intends even now not judgment, but salvation. On the cross, God's Son took all human guilt upon himself, bore it, and atoned for it. God's Son has entered into all of the darkness of evil to enlighten the dark night of sin, to conquer the power of evil, and to burst the bonds of death. This is the truth that makes us free. It forgives all who repent and believe. This is why we sing, "In the cross is salvation, in the cross is victory, in the cross is hope."[9]

We live our lives in the shadow of the cross. It is the cross that first reveals to us the whole truth about our life: it is a finite, broken, and disabled life. It a life that can be guilty of wrongs and one always in need of mercy and reconciliation. But in the end, it is a life lived in the hope of eternal life.

GOD AND SUFFERING (REFLECTION FOR GOOD FRIDAY)

The question of "God and suffering" is as old as humanity. In the face of the abyss of suffering that is everywhere in the world, how is it possible to believe in a good and merciful God?

Many answers to this question have been proposed. Rightly, all of them have been rejected as too easy, too glib. So the question remains open, like a gaping wound that never heals. Neither do we Christians have a theoretical answer ready at hand that we can simply recite. Whoever thinks he has such an answer should ask himself whether he knows what he is talking about. But what we Christians do have is a model for practice, the very practice of God.

For this, let us turn our eyes to the suffering Jesus Christ. What is his suffering? The uniqueness of the suffering of Jesus lies in his experience of abandonment by God on the cross. No one was more conscious of his union with God than was the Son of God become flesh. Here is how theologian Hans Urs von Balthasar puts it: "No one can...experience abandonment by God as deeply as the Son. This is the deepest suffering that is possible: to know, to experience who God is, and then to lose that God (seemingly forever)."[10] To suffer this deeply is to lose all ground under one's feet. To suffer this deeply is, literally, to experience hell.

Yet the suffering of Jesus Christ is not only the deepest possible suffering; it is, at the same time, an act of the greatest surrender and love, the surrender of the Son to the unfathomable will of the Father, but also an act of the greatest devotion of the Father to the Son and to the world. "For God so loved the world that he gave his only Son" (John 3:16). Any image of a God "enthroned above" in heaven and looking down undisturbed at the suffering of the world is forever shattered by the cross. God takes the suffering of the world to heart; those who suffer in the world are in the heart of God.

In the suffering and death of Jesus Christ on the cross, suffering is not done away with in the world. But it is challenged and deprived of its meaninglessness. It becomes an expression of the deepest love, of humanity's love for God and of God's love for human beings. God did not send his Son into the world only to suffer, and through that suffering to change the world. Jesus Christ came so that we would have life and have it in its fullness. For that reason, Jesus fought against suffering wherever he encountered it. He healed the sick, freed human beings from their anxieties, delivered the lonely from their abandonment. And he did more: he placed himself completely on the side of the suffering. The suffering of Jesus is understandable only in this light. The passion of Jesus Christ is the final consequence of his devotion to others. His suffering is the price of his love. Yet love is stronger than death. Jesus's love was not destroyed by death. The way of Jesus did not end in the darkness of Good Friday, but led into the bright light of Easter morning.

In the end, suffering is part of our mortal existence. As finite and mortal creatures, we human beings do not have complete control over our lives: we must also suffer our lives. We were born and must die. In suffering we come face-to-face with our frailty and transience. Even if we are spared illness and distress in our physical life, we will not escape death—no matter how much we try to ward it off. Something of the truth of our life and of human existence is revealed in our suffering; our life becomes a lie when we flee from this truth, when we repress awareness of suffering and death. So, our suffering pulls us back from all that is insignificant and returns us to the core of our existence.

Only when we ourselves live in solidarity with those who suffer may we speak to others about the mystery hidden in their suffering. Only when we, like Jesus, commit ourselves to others in solidarity can we become witnesses to the hope that Jesus Christ has risen beyond all the suffering of the world and thus given us the strength to live.

CHAPTER FIVE

NEW LIFE
(REFLECTIONS FOR EASTER)

"DO NOT BE AFRAID" (EASTER VIGIL, YEAR A: MATTHEW 28:1–10)

When Jesus was condemned and nailed to the cross on Good Friday, terror, fear, and trembling had also gripped his disciples. In losing him, his disciples lost the whole meaning and content of their lives. They lost the ground under their feet. Then they are told, "Do not be afraid....He is not here" (Matt 28:5–7). Do not expect to find him in the grave where you are looking, there where your dreams were also buried with him. "He is risen." He lives.

Do not be afraid! "He is not here." That is also the message of this Easter night. Our happiness and fulfillment are not to be found in the places in which we usually seek them.

Expectations of earthly salvation have deceived us. And yet this does not leave us lost. With its message of "He is risen," Easter brings a new perspective, a new hope to our lives. "Risen from the dead" means this: He lives forever and always with God—God, the fullness of life, who also wants to give us such fullness of life. We will be saved forever and eternally at home. Yes, even in the suffering and death of Jesus, we do not fall from God's hands. With him and through him, lasting justice will be established and the longings of our hearts will be satisfied.

"Do not be afraid!" This is not a cheap recourse to the hereafter. It is an impulse, an encouragement already for our life here and now; it is a confidence that our lives will not fail in the end, giving us courage to live now today; and it certainly draws us to work for life, to protect life, to preserve life, to promote life wherever we can. Since God is a friend of life, we too may and must be friends of life.

Resurrection begins here and now. It begins wherever people again take courage, wherever people bravely and patiently go their way and shoulder their cross instead of hanging their heads in despair. Resurrection begins whenever people who have not spoken to each other for months or years approach each other, speak with each other, extend a hand to each other, and try again to go further with each other. Resurrection begins whenever people overcome their egoism, turn to other persons to console them and help them cope. Resurrection begins whenever, privately or publicly, we act for decency, justice, and human dignity, and wherever we oppose fashionable prejudices for the sake of truth and its honor. Resurrection begins wherever and whenever we come together to celebrate the Eucharist. "We proclaim your death, O Lord, and profess your resurrection until you come again": these are the words we sing or say at the proclamation of faith during the Eucharistic Prayer.

Every Eucharist is a celebration of Easter, a source of life, of strength, of encouragement and hope. Let us make the Sunday Eucharist ever more the source and summit of our Christian life. Precisely today, when so many have lost a sense of hope, we need this celebration of new life. For each time we celebrate, we are told, "Do not be afraid." "He is risen." He is alive and wants you, too, to have the fullness of life. You will live, live in eternity.

"THOSE WHO BELIEVE DO NOT TREMBLE" (EASTER VIGIL, YEAR A: MATTHEW 28:1–10)

At Easter, something decisive has also happened for us and to us: a new life has begun for us, a new future has opened up to us.

The Apostle Paul writes, "All of us who have been baptized into Christ Jesus were baptized into his death....so that, just as Christ was raised from the dead by the glory of the Father, so we too might walk in newness of life" (Rom 6:3–4): we should be dead to sin, but alive for God. We should leave behind a life that values only what is worldly and that acts according to worldly standards and so loses and entangles itself in the world. We should leave behind a deadly life that will surely end in death, and rise to the only kind of life that has a future now and forever; we should open ourselves up to a life for God.

The first words spoken to the disciples who had been terrified and intimidated by the events of Good Friday were these: "Do not be afraid" (Matt 28:5). Pope St. John XXIII put it this way: "Those who believe do not tremble."[1]

Fear is a basic sensitivity of human beings, so said a great philosopher centuries ago.[2] We all feel as if the ground is shifting under our feet, as if things just cannot not go on as they have gone and continue to go.

"Do not be afraid." For the risen Jesus goes before us. Therefore, let us set out and tell the good news to his and our sisters and brothers. There really is no alternative to this message of new life. No one has anything better and more forward-looking to say to us. Let us pass this faith on to our children and grandchildren. There is nothing more important for their lives than such hope.

At the same time, let us accept this new situation as our own personal challenge; let us seek to form it according to Easter hope. Let us not turn fearfully back to the past, but turn with confidence to what is ahead. Whoever believes the Easter message and knows herself to be called in baptism to a new life knows this: there certainly are catastrophes and there is the frightening darkness of death, but these do not have the last word. At Easter, God has promised us a new future. God has given us the gift of hope, a hope that gives us courage not only to hang on to the past but to set out confidently into the future. It is a hope that is not fixed only on earthly standards, but opens itself to God and God's Word—to God who promises us life. Let us not, then, rely on the brittle standards of this world. Instead of holding ourselves to the expectations and promises of this world, let us rely on the promises of God and God's Word, as they were in the beginning, are now, and will be forever. As persons who have been baptized, let us try to walk into new life.

NEW LIFE (EASTER VIGIL, YEAR C: LUKE 24:1–12)

"Why do you look for the living among the dead? He is not here, but has risen" (Luke 24:5–6). Such is the message of Easter, the message on which everything stands or falls. The stone rolled away from the tomb of Jesus is the foundation stone on which the church is built, and on which our life and its meaning are also founded. For the Apostle Paul, too, the whole Christian faith stands or falls on the resurrection.

Without this reality, he says in his first letter to the church in Corinth, faith is empty, futile, worthless (1 Cor 15:17).

Everything, then, depends on Easter: the entirety of our Christian faith, the entirety of our hope, the entire meaningfulness and purpose of our human life. Easter is about these questions: What is our humanity worth? For what may we hope?[3] Indeed, may we hope at all, or must we bury as dead our hope for meaning, for justice, for lasting fulfillment and eternal happiness?

Easter is about the purpose and hope of our lives. Even more foundationally, Easter is about our questions of who God is and who God is for us. Sacred Scripture tells us this: God is life, and the fullness of life. From all eternity God has wanted life, not death. From all eternity, God wants our salvation, our happiness, our peace, and our joy, life, eternal life, and the fullness of life. According to God's will, life in its fullness is the beginning and end of everything.

Easter is the final promise that God will lead our lives to success. God's faithfulness reaches beyond our earthly life; it embraces both life and death. God is faithful and justifies our longing and hope for life, for meaning and lasting fulfillment: God himself has implanted these within us. God loves us with an undying love and wants us to be with him; God wants us in both body and soul. And so, for those who believe, death is not the final station but a gate that opens to new and eternal life, to life with and in God. We pray these words in the Preface of Masses for the Dead: "Indeed, for your faithful, Lord, life is changed not ended."[4] If this were not so, we would have to doubt not only God's faithfulness, but also God's justice. Hope for a new, eternal life both in and beyond death is at the center of Christian faith in God and of the Christian understanding of human beings: it is indissolubly linked with both of these.

New Life

For us Christians this life of ours is not a waiting room, a place where we wait impatiently until the door to eternity finally opens. New life arises right here in the middle of this life. Paul tells this to us: "So you must also consider yourselves dead to sin and alive to God in Christ Jesus" (Rom 6:11).

A Christian's whole life should be an Easter life. The resurrection should thus become present in the midst of our daily lives. Whenever someone accepts her destiny, patiently and bravely bearing and carrying on with a kind of deep trust; whenever parents give the new life of their child a chance, accepting and raising it in spite of the difficulties and obstacles; whenever, after a long period of silence and perhaps even hostility, lack of contact is broken through and persons again come into communication and reconcile themselves to each other; whenever one breaks free from a broken life and begins anew—in these and in many other similar situations, resurrection begins to happen in the midst of everyday life, and hope breaks in. Easter happens whenever human beings overcome fear; whenever people do not get stifled by their petty preferences or fight fanatically for their own ideas; whenever they can let go; whenever they become free enough to see others and to search in hope for something new.

To be able to live in this Easter faith and persist in a life of such Easter practices, we need communities of support and of faith. The presence of the risen Lord and of new Easter life are intensified in a particular way in the communal celebration of the Eucharist: "We proclaim your death, O Lord, and profess your resurrection until you come again." Every Sunday should be a celebration of Easter. And so, we should be Christians who hold Sundays sacred and who know that celebrating Sunday as the Lord's Day has been central to Christian faith since apostolic times.

God's Spirit Creates Living Spaces (Easter Vigil, Years A, B, C: Ezekiel 36:16–28)

A home can be very empty and cold if it is not enlivened by people. Even objects and things that I need seem hard and lifeless if they are not given with care and with love. We can build an external structure with our money, but not a living space and certainly not the life that can fill it.

> I will take you from the nations, and gather you from all the countries, and bring you into your own land. I will sprinkle clean water upon you, and you shall be clean from all your uncleanness, and from all your idols I will cleanse you. A new heart I will give you, and a new spirit I will put within you, and I will remove from your body the heart of stone and give you a heart of flesh. I will put my spirit within you, and make you follow my statutes and be careful to observe my ordinances. (Ezek 36:24–27)

Human hearts harden and turn to stone when they are closed off to the Spirit, or when they turn away from the Spirit. Then the demonic spirit reigns. That spirit does not bring life, but death and ruin.

And so, human hearts need cleansing, constant renewal, and conversion. This is not so much a question of psychological growth as of realizing that God alone can take from us our heart of stone and give us a heart of flesh. We must ask God to send God's Spirit upon us, so that we will want to live by his words and commandments because we recognize in them the way to true life.

It is this Spirit of God who gives rest in the midst of restlessness, who breathes a cool breeze in the midst of heat, and who gives comfort in suffering and death. Without the Spirit, nothing is safe and sound in us; for the Spirit warms what has become cold and hard, melts what has frozen within us, and brings life back into the desert.

God's Spirit and breath is a deep breath: God's Spirit overcomes our tiredness and resignation. All positions of authority in the church have the responsibility to support, sustain, and promote life. For houses themselves are not living spaces. Those who have been filled with the Holy Spirit and thus given "a heart of flesh and not of stone" create living spaces in which all can live.

THE GIFT OF FREEDOM (EASTER SUNDAY, YEARS A, B, C: COLOSSIANS 3:1–4)

"Christ is risen"…"the clouds have disappeared."[5] But is this true? May we really proclaim this in the face of the world's misery and injustice? Can and should I really believe this? The first disciples also had their questions and doubts. We may ask our questions; we need not suppress them.

Nonetheless, such faith is not at all absurd. The miracle of Jesus's resurrection is God's response to a longing that is indelibly engraved in our hearts. This longing corresponds to a dream, even more, to a hope that is in us as human beings. Do not we, too, feel and think this sometimes—that it cannot go on like this forever? It cannot be true that it is always those with the sharpest elbows who win in the end. And it cannot be true that violence, lies, and hatred have the upper hand in the end. Death and all the fearsome powers of death cannot have the last word. Could we really accept that, at the end of it all, what we have done and suffered in our lives means nothing and that our lives end in a wasteland of nothingness?

God has exposed all the evil powers of death, hatred, and violence that threaten and oppress life. God has disarmed, mocked, and put them to shame. God has shown once for all time that life, justice, and truth have the last word. The way to heaven, the way to life is no longer closed off, blocked, and barricaded; it is open. "Set your minds on things that are above, not on things that are on earth" (Col 3:2).

According to Jesus, it is not the small-minded who are free, those afraid of coming up short and so desperately marching along with and participating in every new thing. It is the generous who are free, those who have the nerve and civil courage to swim against the tide. The one who is really free sees others beyond himself, not egoistically looking only after himself. The one who is really free can look beyond her own horizon and work for others. Those who are really free have eyes and ears, heads and hearts free for the needs, questions, and concerns of others; they have hands open and ready to help others. To be really free is to commit oneself to a greater cause, like life, freedom, and justice. Love is true freedom.

Jesus Christ, who has gone before us in his resurrection, has freed us from a dogged, hopeless production mentality. He has already "produced" everything for us. We can rely on him. To him and through him we can pray, and whoever prays knows that prayer frees us from despair and fear about our lives. Prayer always gives us new confidence, hope, and inner peace. It gives us courage and strength really to live. To pray with sincerity and to pour out one's heart before God is a gift of Christian freedom.

"But God..." (Easter Sunday, Years A, B, C: Acts of the Apostles 10:34a, 37–43)

"You put him to death, but God raised him on the third day" (see Acts 10:39–40). This is the center of the apostle Peter's Easter preaching. This sentence contains an accusation and a word of triumph, both at the same time. It contrasts the evil actions of human beings with the healing powers of God.

First, Peter reminds us that Jesus of Nazareth came in the power of the Holy Spirit, that he went from village to village, from city to city, preaching the coming of the reign of God and doing good and healing many of their illnesses. "God was with him" (Acts 10:38). But this worthiest, most just, and holiest of all human beings, who preached and lived only nonviolence, met harsh rejection and blind hatred. The darkest powers of untruth and violence did not rest until they killed him. They subjected him to an unjust trial, mocked and tortured him, and finally hanged him on the gallows of the cross, where after three hours he died a miserable death.

Yet this bitter indictment is not at all the fullness of Peter's Easter preaching. It is only one side of the story, however dark and sinister. The apostle sets a strong counterpoint to it: "But God raised him on the third day." He sets the saving deeds of God over and against the evil and hateful acts of human beings. God has brought about an unexpected upheaval, an all-out reversal, creating a fundamentally new situation. God has found a way out of the hopelessly broken situation of humanity in which the powers of evil always thwart our good attempts. By raising Jesus from the dead, God has saved us from the powers of evil and has given us a new beginning. In the end, what is proven right and victorious are not hatred and violence, but reconciliation and love; not lies, but truth; not death, but life.

For Christians, the message of Easter reigns: "But God raised him on the third day." This brings a new dimension into play. This articulates for the first time the full truth and the actual reality that we often forget or neglect in our merely human logic.

This "but God..." is the message of the living God as the reality that embraces and surpasses all other realities; of the

God who embraces both life and death, and who thus can bring new life even from death; of the God who wants us to live and not die, and who has raised Jesus as the first of those awakened from the sleep of death. With this living God, we are given a foothold in every situation; with this God, hope is always possible. In raising Jesus from the dead, God has shown his divine nature.

This "but God…" brings us yet one more important perspective. It says to us that, on account of the resurrection of Jesus from the dead, there is always a way out and that a new beginning is always possible, even when we totally lose our way and can see no human way forward. This is why Peter speaks of forgiveness of sins in his Easter preaching. At first this sounds terribly outdated to us. But is it really so? Does entanglement in sin and guilt really no longer apply to us? Even today, must not a final note be sounded and a new beginning be given to us if we are to escape from the vicious circle of evil, lies, and violence? But this is precisely what is meant by a word of forgiveness. Real reconciliation and peace are possible only if the recreating grace of God's reconciliation and peace take root in us. Only human beings who have peaceful hearts can be peacemakers. Only people who have been redeemed can speak a freeing word to others; only such persons can bring reconciliation where hatred and hostility have reigned.

Believing Thomas (Second Sunday of Easter, Years A, B, C: John 20:19–31)

The gospel story of the encounter of the risen Jesus with the apostle Thomas gives us much to think about. Because Thomas at first questioned the truth of Jesus's resurrection, he is often referred to as "doubting Thomas." But, in truth, we should speak of "believing Thomas." For, in the end, Thomas knelt down before Jesus and said, "My Lord and my God" (John 20:28). That is, he came to faith.

In matters of faith, this Thomas is very much like us. At first, he says, "Unless I see the mark of the nails in his hands, and put my finger in the mark of the nails and my hand in his side, I will not believe" (John 20:25). And this is just the way we, too, think and speak. We want to see for ourselves; we want tangible evidence. What matters most to us is what we can see, touch, observe. We want something in our hands. But faith in God, in the resurrection, and in eternal life are not things we can see or touch, or have tangible evidence of. Aren't we all a little like doubting Thomas?

It is written that, out of fear of the Judean leaders, Jesus's disciples had gathered behind locked doors. They feared that what had happened to Jesus would happen to them, that they, too, would meet their fate. There is also fear among us. For many today, fear is virtually their trademark. And there is reason for this. Many are afraid that they will lose their jobs. Many others must live in fear of being deported, and so they do not know how to go about their lives. Mothers are often afraid for their children. Others are afraid for their own health or for that of their relatives.

So, aren't we not only like doubting Thomas with his doubts, but also like the disciples who locked themselves behind closed doors out of fear? Let us reflect, then, on the response that Jesus gives! Let us ask how he helped Thomas and the disciples and how he continues to help us now!

Jesus does not respond to the doubts of Thomas by giving him definitive proof. It does not happen that Thomas actually grasps or touches Jesus. Much more significant and even decisive is the personal encounter between Jesus and Thomas.

It is also like this for our faith. We cannot prove it. Many are so concerned to have proof that they look and ask for miracles. But Jesus says to us that we should not seek after miracles and signs. In the end, Jesus says. "Blessed are those who have not seen and yet have come to believe" (John 20:29).

We cannot even have proof of things in our everyday lives. I can have indications but not proof that someone loves me and is faithful to me. If a couple seeks proof of such love, it only means that their love is long dead. It is just this way with faith. There are many indications that God is present, indications that God cares for us each day and in ever new ways. There are traces of God's presence in our lives. And these are enough for us to entrust ourselves to God. To believe means this: trusting God, and entrusting our lives and ourselves to God. Anyone who tries to do this will find herself getting a foothold in life; such a person will experience that he stands on solid ground and has built on a sure foundation.

Faith does not work like a sudden miracle. It does not simply blow our questions and worries away. But faith does drive away fear. It takes away our sense of groundlessness. One with only a little faith is left with one's fears, for such a person does not trust God and God's providence. Such a person is left with no sense of the ground under his feet. Much of our anxiety, doubt, and distress come from our not truly believing.

Presumably all of this was also going on for Thomas as he was met by Jesus. Presumably Thomas also felt some shame about his doubts and initial lack of faith.

The risen Jesus shows Thomas the wounds in his hands, his feet, and his side. They did not disappear with the resurrection; they are still there. But they were transfigured. So will it also be with those things that we have suffered in this life. Everything that we have done and suffered for the sake of love will endure forever. It will enter into the eternal transfiguration. That is true of our daily, often difficult work, of our care for our children and family, of our readiness to be helpful and hospitable to others, of the sacrifices that we make, and of the sufferings and illnesses we must bear. The promise of Easter applies to our entire life.

If we believe as Thomas did, then we know this: Easter and resurrection are not matters for some time in the near or distant future. Easter does not first occur after our death. It begins here and now. The whole life of a Christian can and should be an Easter life.

"PEACE BE WITH YOU!" (SECOND SUNDAY OF EASTER, YEARS A, B, C: JOHN 20:19–31)

"Peace be with you!" (John 20:19, 21). The disciples were filled with fear as Jesus spoke these words. They did not dare to show themselves in public, but were gathered behind locked doors. They did not know how they could go on after Good Friday. In the midst of this difficult situation, Jesus says, "Peace be with you!" Jesus thus wishes them the very thing that we human beings most need: peace. Now, peace is not only the greatest good on earth; for Jesus and the whole Old and New Testaments, peace is the essence of the salvation and happiness that God wants to give and has given us through the death and resurrection of Jesus.

Peace means no one is excluded, no one is abused, and no one is expelled from her homeland. Peace also means people living and working together in a justly ordered society, people accepting and respecting one another as human beings. Peace presupposes justice for all and the protection of human rights. We are to live at peace, then, not only with our friends and not only with those of our own nation.

And peace has an even deeper root. It begins in our own hearts. For it is there that our evil thoughts and intentions arise; it is there that hatred and thoughts of revenge arise and then lead to injustice. But it is also there that the righteousness and benevolence that we ought to model for one another arise. In the end, there can be peace only if we carry it in our own hearts, if we root out all thoughts of hatred, envy, resentment, and revenge, if we live in peace with ourselves and with God.

God has made such a peace with us through the cross and resurrection of Jesus. God has forgiven the guilt of us all and given us a new beginning. What is now important is that we Christians show ourselves to be people of peace. It is no accident that Jesus blesses peacemakers in the Sermon on the Mount: "Blessed are the peacemakers, for they will be called children of God" (Matt 5:9). These words are not only about grand policies. The work of peace begins in families, in our workplaces and neighborhoods, in our communities, and anywhere else that people come together. Whenever a Christian encounters another human being, her first message must be this: "Peace be with you!"

The gospel reports to us how the risen Christ appeared to the frightened disciples and, in particular, how he encountered the apostle Thomas. At first, Thomas did not want to believe that Jesus was alive. But his doubts were overcome when he met Jesus himself. Suddenly he realized that it is not death and the forces of death, not hatred, lies, and violence that have the last word. God is a living God and a friend of life; in his love, God also wants us to love. Yes, even beyond our death, God wants to give us eternal life. And so, in the end, we Christians need not be afraid; we can trust God, and we can trust in life. We can trust that, in the end, it is not hatred and violence that have the upper hand. Rather, it is much more the good that we do and the love that we practice that will be blessed and rewarded by God.

Like the apostle Thomas, let us again fall to our knees

before God who has revealed all of his love to us in Jesus, and let us exclaim, "My Lord and my God!" (John 20:28). In addition to the Sunday Eucharist, let us also join together in prayer in our families. Doing so will bring us together; it will bring us strength, consolation, and hope.

"RECEIVE THE HOLY SPIRIT" (SECOND SUNDAY OF EASTER, YEARS A, B, C: JOHN 20:19–31)

After Good Friday, the disciples lived in fear and terror. Out of sheer fear they came together only behind locked doors. They had to experience how their master, who had preached and lived nothing but love, was subjected to hatred and violence, and cruelly put to death on the cross. On Good Friday, the powers of death, lies, and violence prevailed over life, truth, and love. The entirety of our world's lack of inner peace was revealed.

But in raising Jesus from the dead, God initiated the great change. At Easter, God showed that life and not death prevails. God insured that truth prevails over lies, and that love prevails over hatred and violence. God gave the powers of peace an entryway into our tempestuous world. God gave us peace.

And so Easter is the foundation of our hopes for peace. For God is a God of life and of peace. Jesus Christ, our risen Lord, is our peace. Whoever believes in him may have courage and confidence that peace will have the last word. Whoever believes in Jesus Christ knows that he has no reason to give up. Whoever believes in him finds strength to commit herself to work for peace and justice. The Apostle Paul calls out to us: "If God is for us, who is against us?" (Rom 8:31).

After Jesus greeted his disciples with the words "Peace be with you," he breathed on them and said, "Receive the

Holy Spirit. If you forgive the sins of any, they are forgiven them" (see John 20:21–23). The power to forgive sins is the great gift of the risen Lord to his disciples.

This Easter narrative tells us that what matters is not only the outward peace of the world, however important that is. The gospel reminds us that there can be peace in the world around us only if peace has first found a place in our hearts.

For, in the end, peace and the lack of peace are decided in our hearts. It is sin that destroys the peace that God has given our lives. It is sin that brings lies, hatred, injustice, and violence into the world. And so sin is the root of the world's discontent and lack of peace. Only when the spirit of sin, the spirit of egoism, lies, hatred, and violence is expelled from our hearts; only when God's Holy Spirit moves in our hearts, can peace rule in the world.

And so, peace begins with us; peace begins in our own hearts. We must purify our own hearts again and again; we must again have our sins forgiven in the Sacrament of Penance. And we must pray again and again, "Come, Holy Spirit, giver of life, and fill us with your power."[6]

At first, Thomas could not believe in the miracle of the resurrection and the possibility of a new beginning. He wavered and doubted. But he came to faith when the resurrected one encountered him. He fell to his knees and said, "My Lord and my God" (John 20:28). Only through a personal encounter with Jesus Christ did he become a witness to and instrument of new life and peace.

This same Thomas tells us what matters in the Christian life. He tells us where we can find the strength to live as Christians in this world. We too must encounter the risen Lord. Yet, the same kind of bodily encounter with him that Thomas had is not possible for us. We are not able to touch and feel Jesus Christ as he did. But we too can encounter him concretely and receive strength from him. We encounter him in his word. We encounter him in prayer. We encounter him in the sacraments, and especially in attending and receiving communion in the Eucharist. And, not at all least, we encounter him in our sisters and brothers, especially in those who are in need. Jesus himself tells us, "Just as you did it to one of the least of these who are members of my family, you did it to me" (Matt 25:40).

THE PEACE THAT THE SPIRIT GIVES (SECOND SUNDAY OF EASTER, YEARS A, B, C: JOHN 20:19–31)

Jesus overcomes the barriers of fear; he passes through the closed doors into the midst of his disciples, and speaks his greeting of peace: "Peace be with you" (John 20:19, 21). He gives them the Holy Spirit as his gift of peace.

In the Bible, *peace* (*shalom*) is an all-embracing word of salvation and a basic symbol of hope. Peace is much more than the absence of war, though this is already something important. But in the Bible, *peace* means far more than this. *Peace* means that everything (human beings, nature, all of creation) is safe and whole. All forms of estrangement—from God, from our fellow human beings, from nature—are abolished. All brokenness, enmity, and lack of reconciliation are overcome. And, not at all least, all that is not peaceful in our own hearts is calmed. This message of peace is what we all long for and, more importantly, what we all need. Peace is the greatest good.

For the Bible, the message of peace has an indispensable prerequisite: peace in the world is impossible without peace with God. Without our being reconciled with God, worldly reconciliation is impossible. For God is the source and goal of all reality; God is the foundation and goal of our life.

SEASONS OF GRACE

When God fades away, all the lights go out; when our
foundation in God is abandoned, everything else collapses
and we are left with nothing but fragments and broken pieces
in our hands.

From all eternity, God's Spirit is the bond of love and
unity between the Father and the Son. The Spirit brought
the cosmos into existence out of chaos; without the Spirit,
everything falls back into chaos. The Spirit forgives our sin
and saves us from the chaos caused by sin. The Spirit heals
the wounds and scars of sin, and gives us new peace, comfort,
serenity, and security. The Spirit leads us into the new creation, the reign of peace, justice, truth, and love.

Only a renewed openness to God's Holy Spirit can save
us from chaos. Only the Holy Spirit, which encompasses and
permeates everything, can change the face of the earth; the
Spirit alone can turn human hearts toward peace. Only the
Spirit can give us lasting peace. At Easter, Jesus Christ promised his disciples that this Spirit would remain with them. His
word "Receive the Holy Spirit" (John 20:22) is still valid and
effective in our world today. It is important to know this. This
faith conviction about the Spirit's ongoing presence takes
away our darkest fears and gnawing doubts. Today, we are no
more godforsaken or godless than human beings ever were;
we live in the ongoing presence of the Holy Spirit. And because
God's Spirit remains with us, we may speak our own joy-filled
yes to our times, our church, and our lives. If we look openly,
we will realize that God's Spirit is working all over the world—
wherever human beings seek truth; wherever they find new
hope and dare to live their lives; wherever they break out
of the prison of their egos and take steps toward reconciliation; wherever they make peace among individuals, nations,
and religions; wherever they work for a better, more just, and
more merciful world. There are more such people than we
usually realize, and it is through them that the Spirit of God

is at work even outside the walls of the church to renew the face of the earth. Despite all our challenges, we may say yes to our time: today, too, is the time of the Spirit!

Walking in the Light of Life (Second Sunday of Easter, Years A, B, C: John 20:19–31)

The Gospels do not name any witnesses to the actual event of the resurrection. No one directly saw it, experienced it, or witnessed it. Obviously, it was not an event that could have been photographed or that we can prove today.

Certainly, the tomb was empty. All the biblical accounts say this, and we have no reason to doubt the truth of these reports. But, in and of itself, the fact of the empty tomb does not mean much. Jesus's body could have been reburied elsewhere or stolen in a fraudulent way. So, by itself, the empty tomb is no proof of the resurrection. But for those who believe in the resurrection of Jesus, it is a clue about and a sign of the mighty works of God to which, according to the Gospel, we cannot "cling."[7]

But what we can hold on to is the faith testimony of the first women and men who believed in the resurrection. They were anything but easygoing dreamers, escapists, and tellers of tales. They were realists who had been dealt a harsh blow by Good Friday. Mary Magdalene is desperate; she stands there weeping. The other disciples are filled with fear and agitation; they dismiss as empty gossip the Easter message told them by the women: that the one whom the Roman and Jewish leaders together had nailed to the cross and killed was now raised by God; that God had allowed him to appear to them (see Acts 10:39–41). We have seen him, the women said; he is no longer dead, but alive. Not in the sense of having returned to his former life. He lives in a new, transfigured way; he lives with God, and has come to us from God to be with and for us in a new way.

Something dawns on the disciples in their personal encounter with the transfigured, risen Lord: This Jesus whom they followed was right. God has shown him to be right. His complete trust in the power of God was not wrong. God has shown himself to be more powerful than death; God has shown that life is stronger than death, that truth conquers lies.

It is Easter faith that decides whether we will trust more in life than in death and the forces of death. Because of Easter we may walk in the light of life. So, Easter is the deepest and final response to our hope. For, are these not precisely the deepest desires and longings of our lives: to trust life and to walk in the light of life?

The message of Easter gives us confidence and hope. It says to us, in raising Jesus from the dead, God has once and for all time given victory to life, to love, and to truth. We need not live in the shadow of death. For eternal life is promised to us. Let us then renew our friendship with Jesus. For the source of our Easter faith is in a personal encounter with him. Our encounter with him in personal prayer, in the word of Scripture, and in the sacraments is the source of our new life of Easter. Without him we can do nothing (see John 15:6). It is only through and with and in him that we can walk in the light of life.

"WERE NOT OUR HEARTS BURNING WITHIN US?" (THIRD SUNDAY OF EASTER, YEAR A: LUKE 24:13–35)

To begin with, in the Emmaus narrative, we meet two people walking along who have been bound together through common experiences and adventures and are now seeking to clarify their thinking and go further in their search by engaging each other in conversation.

The walk that these two disciples are taking is an image of the life of every single human being. In our own lives, too, there are many such people with whom we share a part of our life journey: people who engage us in fruitful conversation about our experiences and adventures and who often open up to us a new and better perspective on things. They are people with whom we have shared good and happy experiences, but also people who have become companions to us in the darkness of our lives—in the hours in which our questions remained unanswered, our feelings remained scattered, and our experiences remained unclear to us.

The decisive turning point in the journey of these two disciples is initiated in their encounter with the risen Lord. In the middle of the darkness of their disappointment and resignation, something breaks open when they encounter this unrecognized companion. Initially at least, what happens next remains unclear and confusing to these disciples. And yet it is clear that there is a force at work here that is stronger than the vortex of resignation and discouragement that has overcome the disciples. From deep within them a confidence arises in them that this new force will see them through—even if they don't yet know exactly how and why this will happen.

"Were not our hearts burning within us?" In retrospect, this is how they will describe what happened: they experienced their hearts being grasped by something that they would only understand intellectually later, after their eyes were opened in the breaking of the bread.

The experience of the disciples on the road to Emmaus teaches us that when our eyes have really been opened to serious questions of meaning, the response to those questions has already been given deep inside us. In the moment when the disciples recognize Jesus himself in the unknown stranger, it becomes clear to them that in their hearts they had already perceived much earlier with whom they were dealing: "Were not our hearts burning within us while he was talking to us on the road, while he was opening the scriptures to us?" (Luke 24:32).

And yet the example of the disciples also shows us that, by itself, this feeling is not enough to effect the decisive change. Only after their eyes were opened and they were able to interpret what had happened to them were they able to make a conscious decision for a new beginning. Only in this way could the embers of faith, love, and hope that had been lit in their hearts in the encounter with Jesus radiate outward to give new shape to their lives. In that same hour, the disciples got up and returned to Jerusalem as witnesses to the resurrection, to testify to others about what they had experienced on their journey and how they recognized Jesus in the breaking of the bread.

We need such witnesses to the living presence of the resurrected one in our world today more than ever. In a time in which more and more people speak about feeling burnt out because they no longer expect anything or at least anything new in their lives; in a time characterized by a frightening degree of joylessness and often also depression; in our time, we need people who do something with the embers that have been lit in their hearts. For it is only in this way that people of our time will become aware again of the longing that in reality is alive also inside them, even if all too often it is hidden and buried under the ashes of disappointed hopes, failed attempts, and bad experiences.

We can be contagious witnesses to the fire of new life in Jesus Christ only if the embers in our own hearts have not been quenched. And so an essential part of any spiritual life consists in taking care not to lose sight of Jesus Christ as our companion.

Engagement with Scripture is fundamental to a life of communion with Jesus Christ. And so is celebrating the Eucharist in communion with others who have decided to live their lives walking the path of the risen Lord.

OUR OWN EMMAUS WALK (THIRD SUNDAY OF EASTER, YEAR A: LUKE 24:13–35)

Two disciples were walking together on the road from Jerusalem to Emmaus. They were "talking with each other about all these things that had happened" (Luke 24:14). And so much had already happened: the arrest, beating, and crucifixion of Jesus, the betrayal and running away of the disciples, the astonishing news of the women, the report that angels had appeared and announced that he had risen. Yet, in the end, there was only resignation: "It's not worth anything." Clearly, they were not counting on the living and life-giving God. It was as if they had been struck with blindness.

As they walk along, and the unrecognized Jesus walks with them, they stop and are suddenly sad. They stop and talk about what is making them sad. They repeat the whole sad story of Jesus, which is also the story of their own disappointed hope. They reiterate both their fear and their skepticism.

All of this is also part of our own Emmaus walk: we do not simply forget the past and dismiss it as an unfortunate episode. Like the disciples on the road to Emmaus, we, too, must stop and reflect.

On their way, as they stop in sadness and are unable to cope with the cross, Jesus explains the scriptures to them: "Do you not understand?" (see Luke 24:25). Was it not according to the will and plan of God, as already revealed in the prophets, that it should happen this way? Do you not understand that God's ways are not our ways, that they have their own logic, and just in this way are amazing? As soon as the disciples take this in, their hearts begin to burn. They experience a new inner warmth; they catch fire again.

Only the Word of God opens up to us the full meaning of life; it opens up to us the great height and depth, the length and breadth of our existence. In Christian understanding, human life is not barren and impoverished. It can and should be a life of fullness, but it should be a life of complete fullness, which in the end only God can give. Only God is big enough to fulfill the depth of our longing.

Jesus does not simply teach the two Emmaus disciples with words and then leave them on their own. He stays with them. He breaks and shares bread with them. He blesses the bread and celebrates the Eucharist with them. Only then are their eyes opened; they recognize him and turn hurriedly back toward Jerusalem, filled with joy. They join together with the other disciples who had had their own experience in the meantime, one in which they, too, realized what had happened: "The Lord has risen indeed!" (Luke 24:34). He is not dead, but lives.

GIVING WITNESS (THIRD SUNDAY OF EASTER, YEAR B: LUKE 24:35–48)

Two things are always involved in being a witness: perception and agency. One who has not seen, or heard, or understood the importance of an event cannot be a witness to it. And one who does not pass on what she has seen, or heard, or understood is ineffective as a witness.

The apostles and disciples are not at all dreamers so

content with their world that they are able to comfort themselves with fantasies. Their courage is gone; their hearts are full of doubt. But Jesus lets them experience his presence, making them unique witnesses of his resurrection. "You are witnesses of these things" (Luke 24:48), he impresses upon them. And the words of Peter in the Acts of the Apostles ring out like a response: "God has raised him from the dead. To this we are witnesses" (Acts 3:15). Without the unique and irreplaceable witness of the apostles and disciples, we would know nothing about Jesus and his liberating good news. But, for us as for the disciples, this testimony is no release from the task of letting the witnessed reality pervade all of our senses. Without our own experience of faith and without again and again renewing our own encounter with Jesus Christ, we cannot be witnesses. Our faith in what we have witnessed must continue to grow. Testimony presupposes conviction.

The testimony that the disciples and apostles laid down for us is not only the report of a past encounter. It is, at the same time, a testimony to a new understanding of God, of themselves, and of the world—an understanding opened up for them by the risen Lord. As the Gospel tells us: "He opened their minds to understand the scriptures" (Luke 24:45). For Jews, the scriptures of the old covenant are more than a book. They are testimonies to their own story, the beginning of their own deliverance, in and from which they shape their lives. The scriptures are their source of hope for their own lives. When the risen one opens the minds of the disciples to understand the scriptures, he teaches them to see the world and themselves with new eyes. In doing so he opens up to them whole new possibilities for living, and he calls them to open up these possibilities to others as well.

Being a witness to faith is more than a matter of words. Most deeply and essentially it is a witness of life, a witness to the possibility of new life made through living a new life.

We are told with straightforward clarity in the First Letter of John: "Whoever says, 'I have come to know him,' but does not obey his commandments, is a liar, and in such a person the truth does not exist; but whoever obeys his word, truly in this person the love of God has reached perfection" (1 John 2:4–5). The trustworthiness of the witness rests on the fullness of her own life. It is necessary for us to experience something that we can then pass on to others with our words.

"Do You Love Me?" (Third Sunday of Easter, Year C: John 21:1–19)

When he gathers with his disciples, Jesus does not discuss organizational plans, strategies, and structures they will need to implement in order to spread the gospel. He does not focus on what we are to make. His question to Peter is simply this: "Peter, do you love me?" (John 21:15–17). That is the decisive question on which everything hangs, the question that the Lord also puts to us: Do you love me? Do you really trust in me? Is your heart open to me? What moves your heart? For what does your heart long? In the end, to what do you give your heart? This is the decisive question of all times: What is our heart's longing? Does it long at all? Or is it empty and dark, simply going along with the routine of everyday life? Is our longing for God dead or covered over by every manner of obsession? Do we love the Lord, is there a corner in our heart out of which we can say with Peter, "Lord, you know everything; you know that I love you" (John 21:17).

Renewal begins within us, in our hearts. It begins in rekindling love that has grown cold. Have we not often been lukewarm?

Indeed, what does Jesus say to us, precisely now, today? Nothing other than what he said then: Cast your net out again, begin again, do not be afraid or sad (see John 21:6). Do not be discouraged and certainly not panicked. You do not need to run for cover. You do not need to hide; let down your guard and go out to people; cast your net out again. Many more people than you know are waiting for the witness of your faith.

In the end, life is victorious. And so, we can be people of trust and hope, people who put on life, promote life, affirm life. Being Easter people means being people of joy. Being Easter people means being people of love, and sharing the love that we have received.

Just as God is with us and for us, so are we to be people of compassion in solidarity with others, people willing to help ground a new culture of worldwide sharing. We are to be Easter people willing to cast out our nets once again. Easter people—people who put on life, who radiate joy and who know how to share in love—are attractive to others now in our day. People like this will be asked, What gives you such vitality? What is your source of strength?

"Do Not Be Afraid" (Fifth Sunday of Easter, Year A: John 14:1–12)

"Do not let your hearts be troubled," says Jesus (John 14:1). Do not be afraid, and do not worry; remain calm and serene!

"Believe in God, believe also in me" (John 14:1). That is the answer. Rightly understood, it is the solution to all our worries. For our situation, as distressing as we so often experience it to be today, is most deeply a test of faith and a call to faith. It asks us where we place our trust, and on what foundation we seek to build. It forces us to decide: Do we place our trust in what we can see and be certain of? If so, then our situation is quite bad indeed. Or do we take seriously that

God is the deepest reality, embracing all and transcending everything? Do we dare to live completely from and for God? Doing exactly this is what it means to have faith.

How should we do this? What steps should we take, what steps can we take toward this?

The answer to this question is again surprising: "I am the way, and the truth, and the life. Whoever has seen me has seen the Father" (John 14:6, 9). Jesus Christ is the reign of God in person, the concrete form, the embodiment and measure of our life in faith. He is both the image of God and the model of the new, redeemed human being.

This is the strength of Christianity. In the end, that strength is not in its teachings and laws, which are important and have their place, but in a person, Jesus Christ; he calls us to follow him. To know such a concrete, personal response is a grace in our contemporary crisis of orientation, in the confusion of opinions. In sincere humility, we may ask, Where have we been given a better response? Where is there something more convincing?

"The Father who dwells in me does his works" (John 14:10). God both gives us the will and accomplishes the work in us. God has done this in amazing ways throughout the history of the church. How much resistance the church has withstood! How small was the company of those who followed him, but how large the community has become! And this same God is also at work in wonderful ways in the church of our day. Is our trust in God perhaps not strong enough? Do we need more daring courage, more openness to risk-taking for our faith? Are we so overburdened as to seek only our own security? Have we grown lame in faith?

This Spirit of God, as Paul says, drives the whole creation. The Spirit is at work in the groaning of all creation, directing it toward the reign of God, the reign of freedom. The Spirit is active wherever something new is stirring or arising, where even in birth pangs something new comes into the world, comes to light. The Spirit pushes ahead toward the coming reign of God. The Spirit is at work, Paul also tells us, in the praying of Christians, in our lamenting, our shouting, and crying out, in our calling out "Abba! Father!" (Rom 8:15).

Living from the Middle (Fifth Sunday of Easter, Year B: John 15:1–8)

"I am the vine, you are the branches. Those who abide in me and I in them bear much fruit, because apart from me you can do nothing" (John 15:5).

Jesus Christ is the Vine; he is both Source of and Guide to life. He is both Savior and Salvation, the one Mediator between God and human beings, Alpha and Omega. He is the beginning, middle, and end of all we do. In everything we do, we are to remain oriented on him. Sociological, psychological, and pedagogical insights are certainly useful, even absolutely essential. But they cannot be the final measure and ultimate benchmark. Especially in our most difficult situations we must orient ourselves on the measure Jesus Christ has given us, indeed on the one that he in his very person is.

The gospel does not tell us only that we are to orient ourselves on Jesus; it also says that we are to live in and from him. Without a day-in and day-out, personally lived spirituality—specifically, without reading Scripture, praying regularly, and attending Mass regularly, even frequently—we will not be able to live fully. We can do some things without him, without Jesus Christ, but they cannot be of real significance. With him we need not have worries about performing our life tasks. For he is the way, the truth, and the life.

Often it is we ourselves who stand in the way of the gospel, most frequently with our harshly defended, unreasonable ideas, which are closed off to God's greater love. Before we preach the gospel to others, we must let it speak to us in our own lives. Before we show others the way, we must find it ourselves. God wants living witnesses who not only testify with words but whose very lives are a witness. The witness of a life is convincing.

The gospel wants us to go forth and bear fruit—fruit ripened with the juice and strength of the Vine that is Jesus Christ. The church of Jesus is a church for others; it is a missionary church—or it is no longer the church of Jesus Christ.

The Apostle Paul tells us what that means. He says that the only thing that counts is faith working through love (see Gal 5:6). What could the true fruit of faith be except love! Without love, all else amounts to nothing.

The fruit of love expected of all Christians is, above all, a personal way of being and acting. It is an attitude of selfless service and willing surrender. We are not asked to give "something" to those we meet along the way; we are to give ourselves, to make ourselves a gift for others. This is the only way Jesus Christ will come into the lives of human beings. Love accepts others; it bears all things and most of all rejoices over the goodness it encounters. Such love bears great fruit; new life emerges from it.

Bringing Forth Fruit (Fifth Sunday of Easter, Year B: John 15:1–8)

In the gospel, Jesus uses the image of the vine and its branches in order to tell us something important about our lives and our faith. He says, "I am the vine, you are the branches" (John 15:5). We are to bring forth fruit and become a rich wine for others; Jesus himself wants to give us the power to do this.

But what sort of fruit is being spoken about here? Jesus answers this question in the following text from the story of the vine and the branches. He says there, "Love one another, as I have loved you" (John 15:12). And so, the fruit we are to bring forth, the fruit that matters, is love.

Love—that's an impressive word, unfortunately also an often misused word, a cheapened and undervalued word. Yet love is what we all so deeply want and need, what we desire and search for in the church.

We Christians are to pass on the love that comes from God. As Christians, our task is to live this world-changing love of God and bring it to others. Everyone is needed in this work, with whatever gifts God has given her or him.

There are many ways to live this love. Our church tradition speaks of the corporal and spiritual works of mercy. The corporal ones are important: "to feed the hungry, give water to the thirsty, clothe the naked, shelter the homeless, visit the sick, visit the imprisoned and bury the dead." And yet the spiritual works are just as important: "to instruct the ignorant, counsel the doubtful, admonish sinners, bear patiently those who wrong us, forgive offenses, console the afflicted and pray for the living and the dead."

Yet, in order that we not fall into a kind of blind activism, Jesus adds another word in the gospel: "Abide in me, as I abide in you" (John 15:4). The branch does not bring forth fruit by itself! First, the vine sends out strength, nutrients, and life. This means that every good thing that we do, any love at all that we pass along—all of this comes from God. By ourselves we can do nothing. We can only bring forth the fruit that really matters if God works through us and we remain rooted in God. Unselfish care for the poor and the despised, respect for all human beings, especially the foreigners among us, renunciation of domination, reverence for life and creation—all these virtues, which our world needs now more than ever, come from God.

And, thank God, such signs of hope are visible around us. It is simply not true that our world and fellow human beings bring forth only bad fruit. Whenever people experience something of the love of God through the love given them by their fellow human being, the world is changed for them. They become friendlier, more hopeful, and more human.

Thus, it is up to us whether the world will be changed and become what God wants it to be. God gives us strength through his Word, through the sacraments, and through his loving affection for us. Our task remains to bring forth fruit, to spread God's affection even further.

"ABIDE IN MY LOVE" (SIXTH SUNDAY OF EASTER, YEAR B: JOHN 15:9–17)

"Abide in my love!" Jesus spoke these words from his farewell discourse in John's Gospel in the face of his approaching death. "Abide in my love" is thus also Jesus's testament and legacy given to us. In this way, Jesus paraphrases the first and most important commandment: Love God with all your strength, and love your neighbor as yourself.

For, in the end, Jesus wanted to say nothing to us except this: God is love. From all eternity, God has loved all of us with an undying love. From all eternity, God has chosen all of us: God has a dream for all of us. With bands of love, says the prophet, God has drawn us to himself (see Hos 11:4). Jesus came so that we would have life and have it abundantly (see John 10:10). To respond to this love, to abide in it, is the purpose and goal of human life. To give our life for our friends, as Jesus gave his, is our fulfillment and our happiness; it is to find God in our neighbor and to discover there also ourselves. That is a summary of the entire gospel.

Love's only chance is in our committing to live it. And so,

in our situation, we would do well to hold on to this word of the Gospel: "As the Father has loved me, so I have loved you; abide in my love" (John 15:9). This is the only foundation on which we can stand. There is no other. And the path ahead is laid out for us.

We are to abide in the love of God for human beings. We are more and more to explore this love, dwell in it, so to speak, and make room for it in us. This means giving contemplation a place in our lives. It means giving it a more conscious, emphatic, and personal place than it was given in the past—when it was more common, but thus also often a mere routine. When we focus on silence, contemplation, and worship, then our "abiding in love" becomes a counteraccent, deeply needed in our time, to the inhumane hustle and bustle, the speed and often superficiality around us. Many young people are seeking precisely this in our day. And precisely this would do all of us much good. In this way, we can respond to the deepest distress of our time, that of the eclipse of God.

"Abide in love" has yet another meaning. The gospel message says that every single person is wanted by God, is accepted by God, loved by God, made worthy by God. Every human being has a right to live, a right to live in a dignified and humanly fulfilled way. Thus, all distress and all suffering, all poverty and grief are callings from God to us. They are callings for us to serve God in suffering humanity. This is what the gospel means by speaking of bringing forth fruit in love (see John 15:16). Love wants to become fruitful, both naturally and supernaturally.

We are speaking about the promise of love. In the First Letter to the Corinthians, Paul says, All things come to an end. Only love lasts. The Second Vatican Council put it this way: the works of love will also stand forever.[8] In this promise, we may look confidently ahead to the future.

PEACE (SIXTH SUNDAY OF EASTER, YEAR C: JOHN 14:23–29)

In many places, the Bible speaks about peace as a gift of God. In the Old Testament, Yahweh again and again renews his covenant with the chosen people Israel. In doing so, God promises the people his own peace. *Shalom* is the Hebrew word for peace. Even today, one hears this as an everyday greeting among Jews in Israel. The German and English words for peace are only a pale and weak translation for all that *shalom* promises. For *shalom* means that everything is as it should be, that all are contented, that all are in harmony with themselves. It means well-being, a peaceful coexistence of friendship with other human beings, with life, and with nature. But *shalom* also means reconciliation with God and opening oneself to the expansiveness of life.

In the New Testament, *shalom* is the greeting of the resurrected one. He comes into the midst of his disciples and says, "Peace be with you" (John 20:19, 21). "Peace I leave with you; my peace I give to you" (John 14:27). Jesus Christ is the promised "Prince of Peace" (Isa 9:6). And so, human beings attain true peace by being in relationship with Christ.

The peace that Jesus gives is different from the peace given by the world. The peace of the world is completely dependent on outside circumstances: that we are spared from war, sickness, and poverty. The peace of Jesus, on the other hand, rests on a sure relationship with and connection to him, a connection that cannot be destroyed even by outside circumstances of need and suffering. Even in pain and persecution, a person who has entrusted himself to Jesus has peace in his heart. Such a person has peace because she knows that God's Spirit is close to her and that nothing can separate her from the love of Christ and of his Father.

Shalom—peace: in a unique and comprehensive way,

this word describes what Jesus wanted, his very purpose, the center of his preaching and his healing and integrity-restoring interactions with all.

In his presence, people experience that they are finally seen and taken seriously. They are moved from the margins into the center, and so feel able to breathe. When someone turns to people so unconditionally, they can live and begin to realize what life can really be, what kind of love is possible. Jesus changes people both inwardly and outwardly.

People who had been rejected by others receive new courage through him, a new lease on life. Their isolation is broken. Human beings who had been weighed down by sadness discover in his presence the spark and hope that is still in them—faith in themselves and in their fellow human beings. People have a sense of the possibilities of living with others when they discover their law of life, namely, that evil can only be conquered by goodness.

Jesus Christ, the Prince of Peace, also challenges us to be and become peacemakers. "Blessed are the peacemakers, for they will be called children of God" (Matt 5:9). This beatitude from the Sermon on the Mount applies to all of us. Peace begins nowhere else than with us ourselves, in our own hearts—just as wars of hatred and envy have their origins in the hearts of human beings.

THE LORD IS RISEN, HE IS TRULY RISEN (REFLECTION FOR EASTER)

This message is simply incomprehensible and unbelievable. It is so not only for us, but it was also incomprehensive and unbelievable two thousand years ago. Not only members of the Sanhedrin but Jesus's disciples themselves shook their heads in disbelief.

The martyred and crucified Jesus Christ, whose heart was pierced by a lance as he hung on the cross and whose body was laid in a grave newly hewn in the rock, lives. He truly lives.

In death, he went to his Father and our Father, his God and our God, and then he appeared personally to his disciples in a glorified, bodily form. He then sent them out to preach to the whole world this message of the death of death, of the victory of life over death.

This message of the resurrection of Jesus Christ is the basis of our own hope for resurrection.

For what is impossible for human beings is possible for God; not only that, but it has truly happened. Life and not death has been given the last word; love has won the victory over hatred and violence.

Many of us contemporary persons are like a person walking in the desert. The unmerciful sun sears him; he becomes weary, exhausted. In the distance, he sees an oasis that could save him. But he is a modern, enlightened human being who has grown skeptical and who won't let himself be fooled by anything. He thinks to himself, It's a mirage, just something in the air that amounts to nothing. He comes closer to the oasis and sees more and more clearly that there are date palm trees, grass, and, most of all, a spring. But he thinks, This is nothing but a fantasy coming from my hunger, a dream of my half-crazed brain. He takes the bubbling water to be a hallucination. And so, he lies down in the hot sand and dies. Not long afterward, two Bedouins find his dead body. One asks the other, "Can you believe it? The dates are right there and the spring is bubbling, but here he lies dead of thirst. How is it possible?" The other Bedouin responds, "He was truly a modern man!"

Easter is the hope-filled alternative to the spreading hopelessness and despair of our time. At Easter, what is impossible for human beings becomes true and real. At Easter, life and the hope for a full and fulfilled life receive their final validation.

Whoever has faith must dare to enter life and risk living even in the face of death, for God is with us and has dared to enter life with us. It is faith, then, that overcomes fear; it is faith that overcomes faint-heartedness, timidity, hopelessness, despondency, frustration, and resignation. Whoever has faith can dare to live a full life.

The resurrection for which we hope begins already here and now. It begins wherever we rise out of our egoism and our too often narrow-minded interests, whenever we open ourselves to justice and love, wherever we make space for forgiveness and reconciliation. It begins wherever we rise from the grave of our discouragement and weariness, our discomfort and dullness, so that we can dare live with God—for whom all things are possible. Resurrection begins wherever we, here and now, seek the greater and not the lesser things.

THE ASCENSION OF JESUS CHRIST (REFLECTION FOR THE ASCENSION)

"So if you have been raised with Christ, seek the things that are above, where Christ is, seated at the right hand of God" (Col 3:1). When we speak of heaven, even in the secularized and often enough banal language of our day, we mean something more than the sky above the earth. Even for us moderns, the word *heaven* stands for the idea of human fulfillment. Whoever looks up to heaven, whether it be on a bright summer day or on a starry night, senses today as always that what we can see is not everything. The human being is more and wants more than what is right in front of us.

So, heaven is not only for dreamers, priests, and sparrows, as mocking tongues would have it. To speak of heaven raises questions not only about what we human beings have, but more deeply about who we are: questions about what brings happiness and fulfillment. We ourselves cannot give any final answer to questions like these. We can only hope for an answer. But where the deepest longing of human beings, which is for God, is fully granted to us, where it completely fulfills us, that is where heaven is: where God is completely with us and where we finally come completely to God.

The first human being to come fully and completely to God and to be wholly and completely accepted by God was Jesus Christ. The ascension of Christ begins the final fulfillment of human longing. In his ascension, Jesus Christ is established as Lord of the world. He becomes its lasting measure and goal. He will be revealed as such to all at the end of time, when "all the tribes of the earth...will see 'the Son of Man coming on the clouds of heaven' with power and great glory" (Matt 24:30). In the return of Christ, all that began in the incarnation of the eternal Word, that was revealed in his words and actions, and that culminated in his suffering, death, resurrection, and ascension—all of this will be fulfilled.

The fulfillment toward which we walk as pilgrims, the heaven for which we hope, is given to us in Jesus Christ. He is God's gift. This fulfillment cannot be provided "from below." No one climbs to heaven through his own deeds, not even through the best of her deeds. God opens heaven to us in freedom as a gratuitous gift. The whole longing of human history comes to its fulfillment in the event of the ascension. At the same time, an inner historical dynamism is characteristic of this event. We shall enter into it by faith.

Thus, the exaltation of Jesus Christ is at the same time the exaltation of our humanity and our history to God. The message of the ascension of Jesus Christ turns out to be a message of hope, namely, the hope that our life is neither a series of arbitrary, meaningless events, nor a fairytale of vanities; that our life is instead the place in which, with God's help, we build up what we will be in eternity. The ascension of Christ gives us confidence: our earthly history does not end in the dust of the ground and in the wasteland of nothingness, but at the end of the day our history must be a part of the life of the world that is to come.

CHAPTER SIX

THE GIFT OF THE HOLY SPIRIT
(REFLECTIONS FOR PENTECOST)

THE SPLENDOR OF THE OLD AND NEW CREATIONS (VIGIL OF PENTECOST: ROMANS 8:22–27)

We human beings should never allow ourselves to lose the so-called naiveté that sees traces of God in this world and marvels at the miracles of the eruption of blossoms in the spring, in every snowflake of the winter, and, most of all, on every human face. And we should never stop saying and praying with St. Francis of Assisi, "Praised be you, my Lord, with brother Sun and sister Moon, and with all your creatures." We should not be embarrassed to leave our modern and postmodern imprisonments behind us, and simply once again be "religious" in the midst of everyday life; we should allow ourselves to suspect that the world is more than a world, that it contains traces and signs of something beyond itself, beyond us, and also beyond everything that we can "make" (whether for good or, as unfortunately happens all too often, for evil). We should allow ourselves to see in it the splendor that is a reflection of the beauty and glory of our God. We must allow ourselves to learn again the language of the psalms: "O Lord, our Sovereign, how majestic is your name in all the earth! You have set your glory above the heavens" (Ps 8:1). When we celebrate the Eucharist together, however, we are not celebrating the splendor of creation but the splendor of the new creation that begins with Easter and the resurrection.

The splendor of both the old world and the new belong together. For there is a dynamic at work in the world that pushes beyond itself. It is not satisfied with itself. The world cannot be understood only in an immanent way. It groans and sighs within itself, as the Apostle Paul says (see Rom 8:23). Our heart is restless, so says the great church father Augustine. Its finds its rest only in Jesus Christ. The Bible tells us that he is the fullness of time; he is the key, the midpoint, and the goal—the point at which all the efforts of history and culture converge. He heals the wounds of the old creation and, at the same time, brings it to its lasting completeness. He is the "hermeneutical key" for understanding the world, whether in its suffering or its greatness.

For the new creation of Easter is a final and lasting yes to the old creation. It says to us, God is life; God does not want death but life, new and eternal life. God remains faithful to us and to our world. God does not let us fall. God's faithfulness embraces both life and death. Because God loves us with an unending love, God wants us, in both body and soul, to be with him for all eternity; in the end, God wants to be all in all, to transfigure all of reality. Thus, light comes into our world from God and, with it, strength and hope for us to face our concerns and worries in this world. For the promise of a new world is no flight from this world; it is no false consolation. It leads us to take responsibility for this world. And it gives us the responsibility of preserving the splendor of creation as far as we are able, so that our children and our children's children can continue to rejoice in it. As Christians, we are to be advocates for life.

The way to resurrection passes through the cross; so, the church of Jesus Christ, the crucified One, can never step out from under the shadow of the cross. It cannot be the church of only splendor and glory.

In an unexpected and wonderful way, within only two generations, the small group of believers grew into living communities spread across the larger cities of the then known world around the Mediterranean Sea. This miracle repeated itself again and again throughout history. Often enough the church was declared dead, and it was never more persecuted than in the bloody twentieth century.

The Spirit, who brings life and who, at the beginning, formed the world from out of chaos; the Spirit who lives and works in all creatures; the Spirit who grants its own splendor to all creation; this same Spirit raised Jesus from the dead and has opened up the final breaking forth of new life and of the new world. This Spirit summons us to be guardians of and advocates for the splendor of creation, and to be messengers of new life. This Spirit also opens our eyes to recognize again and again the splendor that lies in the world, in Jesus Christ, and in the life of our church.

"RECEIVE THE HOLY SPIRIT" (PENTECOST SUNDAY: JOHN 20:19–23)

"Receive the Holy Spirit" (John 20:22). This is the decisive statement in the gospel of Pentecost; likewise, it is the great gift that Jesus made to his disciples and his church after his resurrection. He promised us the ongoing assistance of the Holy Spirit, even making his church—as Paul put it (see Eph 2:20–22)—the temple of the Holy Spirit.

Faith is suffering from a kind of fatigue in our day. Deeply committed Christians often feel at the margins, their voice and influence having become markedly weaker.

We must discover again the message of Pentecost and count on the reality and efficacy of the Holy Spirit. It is only the Spirit who can help us out of our difficulties. For we need a spiritual renewal. And it is only the Spirit of God who can cause us Christians, the church, once again to become on fire and enflamed for God and God's reign, to become committed witnesses of Jesus Christ. The Spirit alone can give us courage not to lock ourselves behind closed doors, but to step forth freely and go out into the whole world, to reignite the fire of faith, hope, and love.

If we accept the witness of Scripture, then the Spirit is not some strange or special reality beyond or above our world. The Spirit of God is much more the breath and inner strength, the principle of life and soul of all reality. Everything was created by and has existence through the Spirit.

The Spirit of God is at work wherever human beings search for truth and seek justice, wherever they wake up and move outward in search of peace and freedom.

In Jesus's being and activity, in his life, death, and resurrection, the hopes of the Old Testament and the longings of all humanity have been fulfilled: through the action of God's Spirit, the reign of God has broken forth as a reign of freedom and mercy. For Jesus did not keep this Spirit to himself. Dying, he breathed forth the Spirit; after his resurrection, he bestowed the Spirit on the apostles and promised the Spirit's lasting presence: "Receive the Holy Spirit." In and through his Spirit, Jesus Christ remains with and among us as our ascended Lord. He did not leave the world on its own, but wants to lead it to its lasting transformation and fulfillment through the power and strength of the Holy Spirit.

It is a transformation that does not rely on violence, but begins in the changing of human hearts. It is a renewal that does not begin with others but within our own hearts—in love, friendship, patience, courage, hope, and trust.

The Spirit of God is at work wherever there is life, wherever life is awakened and preserved, wherever life reaches beyond itself and strives for meaning and fulfillment. In a special way, we can recognize the traces of the Spirit of God wherever people break out of the trap of their egoism, find love, forgive and pardon others, are good to them, and help them without expecting any return. It is only in such devoted love, and not in constricted self-concern and cramped self-realization, that human beings really find themselves and their fulfillment.

We can only find our deepest and final fulfillment, however, when we are accepted and affirmed completely and unreservedly, when we are fully united in love and friendship with God by the Spirit of God, and are able to share in God's life. Such friendship with God manifests itself as joy-filled praying and reading the scriptures, and it brings with it inner peace, confidence, consolation, hope, and happiness. Not at all least, it also gives strength in suffering and in experiences of injustice, rejection, and persecution; and it gives the courage and generosity to stand up against all adversity for Jesus Christ and his reign.

The Spirit Gives Life (Pentecost Sunday: Acts of the Apostles 2:1–11)

The message of Pentecost that the Spirit of God is a life-giving Spirit is a message of hope for all living things. God is life: everything that exists owes its existence to God. Everything that exists has value that comes, first of all, not in their relation to human beings, but directly from God. This is a message of reverence for all that is and has life, a message of human responsibility for life in this world and for the protection of creation. It is a message especially about human life, including unborn human life, a message of hope for injured, impaired, and disabled life. It is a message about the forgiveness of sins and guilt and of hope for a new creation.

For those who believe in the Spirit of God, our world and life in the world do not end in a wasteland of nothingness; instead they open out into the freedom of the daughters and sons of God in the coming reign of God. Pentecost's message of life is also a message of freedom: "Where the Spirit of the Lord is, there is freedom" (2 Cor 3:17).

Finally, the message of the life-giving Spirit—as a message of life and of freedom—is also a message of peace and unity. The account of the first Pentecost reports that through the coming of the Spirit the confusion of language among people and nations caused at Babel (see Gen 11:1–9) came to an end; it reports that all could understand one another, as the great deeds of God were recounted (see Acts 2, especially 4—11). All who honor the one Father in heaven, profess faith in the Lord Jesus Christ, and are bound together in the Holy Spirit are, no matter their skin color, nationality, or culture, all brothers and sisters in the one family of God.

A lasting order of world peace will be possible only if that peace is grounded in the hearts of human beings themselves. For the roots of hatred, envy, and strife are all in the human heart. Only the holy and healing Spirit can heal the wounds in the hearts of so many people of our time and free us from our numbness. Only the Spirit can fulfill the deepest longings of the human heart. This is what we pray for when we sing *Veni, Creator Spiritus*:

Come, Holy Ghost, Creator blest,
and in our hearts take up Thy rest.
Come with Thy grace and heavenly aid
to fill the hearts which Thou hast made.

"COME, HOLY SPIRIT" (PENTECOST SUNDAY: GOSPEL SEQUENCE)

The traditional hymn *Veni Sancte Spiritus* (Come Holy Spirit) begins with these words:

Come, Holy Spirit, Lord of Light,
From thy clear celestial height.
Thy pure beaming radiance give….

If thou take thy grace away,
Nothing pure in us will stay;
All our good is turned to ill.

Heal our wounds, our strength renew;
On our dryness pour thy dew,
Wash the stains of guilt away.

Bend the stubborn heart and will;
Melt the frozen, warm the chill;
Guide the steps that go astray.[1]

The joyful and liberating message of the gospel of Pentecost is that, after his resurrection, Jesus Christ gave us the saving and sanctifying Holy Spirit, the only source of our hearts' fulfillment. After the bitter events of Good Friday, the disciples were distraught and terrified.

All the hope they had placed in Jesus and in his message

of the coming reign of God seemed to be a deception. It all seemed to be over, everything lost. Then the risen Lord came into their midst and showed them his transfigured wounds as bodily proof that they need not fear. For, by raising Jesus from the dead, God showed that love and not hatred and violence, that life and not death, have the last word. Easter gave final justification to the hope for life, for fulfilled and eternal life.

As a pledge of this victory of life, justice, truth, and love, he breathes on the disciples and bestows the Holy Spirit on them. Through the Spirit, the risen Lord will henceforth keep alive the disciples' memory of him and of his Easter victory; through the Spirit, he will remain present and active in the world; through the Spirit, new life will be forever present in the hearts of believers. The Spirit of God, who at the beginning of creation swept over the face of the waters and transformed chaos into cosmos—this living and active creator Spirit, who orders and guides all things and whose fullness was promised to us at Pentecost; this is the Spirit who heals the wounds of the old world, who sanctifies and fulfills all things, who gives direction and an eternal destiny to all.

Pentecost is the feast of abundance and fulfillment. For the saving work of Jesus, the inbreaking of the reign of life, of peace, and of freedom, comes to its completion at Pentecost. At Pentecost, this good and sanctifying Spirit is given completely to us as help against the imposter, the evil spirit of lies and violence. After Pentecost, the world is no empty and menacing wasteland; instead, a life of inner freedom, peace, and joy becomes possible for all who open their hearts in faith. Through Pentecost, new life has been definitively opened up to us. As another Pentecost hymn, *Veni, Creator Spiritus*, has it:

Come, Holy Ghost, Creator blest,
and in our hearts take up Thy rest.

SEASONS OF GRACE

Come with Thy grace and heavenly aid
to fill the hearts which Thou hast made.[2]

We all yearn for things to be made new, to be different from what they are, for the wounds of the past to be healed, for what had hardened and entrapped us to be broken, for a new beginning to become possible, for all tears to be wiped away and all suffering to come to an end. Indeed, who other than God and God's creating Spirit can overcome what is warped and distorted in the world and in our own lives? Who else can break open our hardened and closed-off hearts; who but the Spirit of God can ultimately fulfill all that we long for in the heights and depths of our hearts?

The Holy Spirit of God is at work wherever human beings break out of our egoism; wherever those estranged from one another break their silence, reach out their hands, and speak to one another. The Holy Spirit of God is at work wherever peace becomes possible between nations or ethnic groups who had been enemies, and wherever breakdowns between spouses or in families are healed. The Spirit is at work wherever someone wakes up from a wasted and narrow life that had shrunken in on itself and begins caring for the larger world around him and engaging with his fellow human beings. The Spirit of God is alive wherever human beings who had lived thoughtlessly and without direction for long periods suddenly begin to seek truth or a deeper purpose in life; the Spirit is present wherever someone who perhaps had spent decades without God and without the community of the church suddenly finds God again in her life or turns herself around and begins a new life. In short, God's Spirit is alive wherever conversion happens and something new springs up.

This is what we ask for when we pray: "Come, Holy Spirit."

THE GIFT OF THE HOLY SPIRIT (REFLECTION FOR PENTECOST)

After the death of Jesus, the disciples had no idea how they could carry on. Their hopes and expectations had been dashed. Everything had turned out differently from how they imagined it would: the one in whom they had hoped and around whom they had built their lives had come to a shameful end on the cross and had left them behind helpless. The disciples were knocked down, depressed, and filled with fear.

But, just then, the unexpected and unimaginable suddenly happens. The one who had been crucified and buried turns out to be the risen one; he is alive and reestablishes communion with his disciples. He walks into the midst of those who, in the middle of their lives, had come to believe themselves completely lost—and he wishes them peace.

In the encounter with the risen one it becomes clear to the disciples: The message Jesus brought was no deception; it is now confirmed by God. It became reality with the resurrection of Jesus. With the resurrection of Jesus, life in God, life in peace and freedom has finally been opened up. God's creating and recreating Spirit, who was at work in raising Jesus from the dead, from now on is promised to all and poured out over all reality. That Spirit seizes the hearts of the disciples so that they become on fire and enflamed for Jesus and for everything he worked for.

Through the encounter with the risen Lord, a whole new phase of life begins for the disciples. The Spirit who had been shared with them and the joy that had broken out in their hearts would not allow them to remain behind closed doors any longer. In the encounter with the risen One, the doors out into the world had been ripped open before the disciples. They were sent out into the world in order to share with others what they themselves had received: the Holy Spirit, who gives life.

From that moment on, this Spirit has become the dynamic force in the church. Through the Spirit, the risen Lord has opened up a new beginning for the community of disciples: he gives the disciples a share in his own divine life. It is also the Spirit who drives the disciples outward to share with others what they have experienced in the depths of their hearts.

The Spirit continues to encounter us believers in the depths of our hearts and open us to others, so that all may be united in the community of the one people of God that embraces all peoples and nations.

The gift of the Holy Spirit is God's response to the deep longing of all human beings for unity and peace. The Spirit is also the response to our longing for inner peace and for the renewal of our church.

A church of those united in a living bond with the risen Lord can again become a sign of salvation for people of our own time; such a church can regain some of the momentum and vigor that shaped its beginning and that, throughout history, led it out to the world in service. Such a church can become an inspiring church, because it has itself been "in-spirited" by the Spirit of Jesus who lives and works in it.

We must never leave off in praying for this Spirit, for only the Spirit can show us the way that leads to our fully being the church of Jesus Christ in the future. With full awareness, then, let us bring our prayer before God in the words of the Pentecost hymn *Veni, Creator Spiritus*, written more than a thousand years ago by Rabanus Maurus (776–856):

> Come, comforter, who guides our hearts,
> You helper, given by the Father.
> Out of you flows life, light, and warmth;
> You give us weak ones strength and courage.[3]

"COME DOWN, O HOLY SPIRIT" (REFLECTION FOR PENTECOST)

The Spirit of God is at work wherever—in the midst of questions and difficulties, failures and conflicts—human beings seek and fight for new and better things, wherever there is more freedom and more justice, peace, and reconciliation. Thus, we can experience something of the mystery of God's Spirit in collaboration, cooperation, and compassion with and for others in this world.

Every Christian has gifts of the Spirit. Here we touch upon the deepest mystery of Christian existence.

Whoever does not live superficially but listens inwardly to her life, experiences something of the mystery of life that cannot be expressed in a clear conceptual way. Such persons experience something of an inner thrust toward goodness and an aversion to evil in their conscience. Many people skip over this quickly. They are so busy with their plans, with pursuing their interests, so concerned with seeking their own advantage, that they have neither time nor space for this inner thrust. Others want to protect themselves against the frightening mystery of life and wall themselves off. They take the broad road by which all travel, instead of going a perhaps lonelier way.

But it also happens that someone suddenly abandons all the customary considerations, although, humanly speaking, doing so is foolish and tactically unwise; that he entrusts himself to another, although he has often been disappointed; that she graciously commits herself to a great cause whose chances of success may not be so rosy; that, in a difficult situation, he does not stand around helpless, but persists bravely and patiently. Anyone who is willing to free herself from the usual generally accepted standards experiences something of the liberating Spirit of Jesus Christ.

The experience of prayer is the truest and deepest experience of the Spirit. This experience requires no great, well-spoken words.

Prayer is a plain, simple saying "Thou" to God as the ultimate and deepest mystery. From it, we receive a confidence, a primal experience of trust that overcomes all our fears of life, because we know ourselves to be absolutely accepted and safe in God's love.

We cannot make such experiences happen, but we can be open and ready for them by creating a space within ourselves for silence. When such experiences are given to us, they can transform our lives, bringing healing and a sense of holiness. Without such in-depth changes, our Christian life can become one of soulless activism. But, when they do happen, they bring true renewal to our church and society. Everything depends on our decision to initiate and continue in such practices of prayer; what is at stake is whether our Christianity remains alive or becomes an empty, soulless enterprise.

> Come, Holy Spirit, Lord of Light,
> From thy clear celestial height.
> Thy pure beaming radiance give....
>
> If thou take thy grace away,
> Nothing pure in us will stay;
> All our good is turned to ill.
>
> Heal our wounds, our strength renew;
> On our dryness pour thy dew,
> Wash the stains of guilt away.

The Gift of the Holy Spirit

Bend the stubborn heart and will;
Melt the frozen, warm the chill;
Guide the steps that go astray....

Give us comfort when we die;
Give us life with thee on high;
Give us joys that never end.

CHAPTER SEVEN

LIVING FROM THE SACRAMENTS

CALLED BY NAME (REFLECTION ON BAPTISM)

In every era, God always needs people like Clare (1194–1253) and Francis (1184–1226) of Assisi—people who dedicate their hands and feet, their eyes, their mouth, and not least their heart, their entire life, to making the world a garden, a vineyard.

Is God no longer calling anyone or, at least, not enough people in our day? Not even close. God has been calling and summoning forth since the beginning of creation. Every single one of us, you and I, is an embodied call from God. For everything that we are and have, all our faculties and abilities, we ourselves as women and men exist because God says, I want you to be. I like you, I love you, I support and lead you, and I send you. Not a single one of us is only a serial number, a little cog in the machinery of the world, a whim of fate or random product. Every woman and man is one of a kind, an original. Everyone is called and has a vocation, and it is up to every single one of us to discern and live it.

At baptism we were all called by our own name. From that day forward we have never been anonymous. It is there that we met Jesus's call to us—just as the disciples were called by him: "You, come follow me" (see Matt 9:9). This call can take many different forms. Laypeople have a vocation; it is not only about priests and religious. Usually one's vocation is related to one's abilities and often to one's profession, for example, as a teacher, nurse, physician, craftsperson, and so forth. Marriage and the single life are vocations, too. We are all called to offer service from our particular position in life.

God also constantly calls individuals in a special way: Abraham, Moses, the prophets, Sarah, Hannah, Esther, Judith, and, above all, Mary. They often struggled long and hard over their vocations. Why me? Can I do this? Should I do it? In the end, they each placed their own plans and wishes, their own life projects at the disposal of God's plan. They freed themselves, let go, and dedicated themselves completely to their vocations. In doing so, they became signs for others, for their own people, and for all humanity. For God says to all of us what he said in calling Abraham: "You will be a blessing" (Gen 12:2). We are called for love and for service.

In most cases, vocations first arise as a quiet knocking at our hearts. At first, they are a small delicate plant that must grow and mature, that must be tended and nurtured, and that can be stifled and uprooted as well. Usually it takes a lengthy period of discerning, testing, talking with others, and having various experiences, and, not least, praying. Disappointments, dry periods, and crises are part of the path, too—but also joy and the great happiness of having found one's direction.

ANOINTING WITH OIL (REFLECTION ON SACRAMENTAL ANOINTING)

Anointing with oil was an important event for people in antiquity. As it still is today, anointing was a remedy in case of injuries—serving to strengthen and refresh the skin and give it luster and beauty. But there are wounds other than physical ones, deep inner wounds to the soul through bitter disappointments and violations. There are also inner experiences of powerlessness and impotence, of helplessness, worthlessness, and insignificance. On the other hand, all true beauty comes from within, from a happy heart and a joy-filled soul. So, it is not only our bodies that need anointing, but also our souls. They, too, long for healing, strength, and luster.

This longing has been fulfilled in Jesus Christ, for *Christ* means "the anointed one."[1] The fullness of the Holy Spirit was given to him. In him, everyone is restored to health and wellness; in him, the fullness and strength of life appeared; in him, the beauty and glory of God has brightened our world.

So, he was sent to preach the good news of God's salvation and glory to the poor, the needy, and the oppressed. He came to heal their wounds, giving them new courage and confidence and filling them with joy. As the Acts of the Apostles puts it, "God anointed Jesus of Nazareth with the Holy Spirit…[and] he went about doing good and healing all who were oppressed" (Acts 10:38).

Jesus continues to move in our midst. After his death and resurrection, he remains present with us. He allows us to share in his anointing with the Holy Spirit. Jesus's anointing continues in the church and in Christians. In fact, Christians are literally "those who have been anointed." The Apostle Paul tells us that God has anointed us, giving us his Holy Spirit in our hearts (2 Cor 1:21–22; see also 1 John 2:20, 27). As Christians, we can participate in Jesus's fullness of the

Holy Spirit; we have been incorporated into the life of the triune God. It is there that our wounds are healed, there that we receive strength and courage to live, there that we are filled with God's glory, joy, and peace.

As a sign of our calling, we were anointed with the oil of the catechumens at our baptism so that the wounds of sin would be healed in us. In baptism and again at confirmation, we were anointed with chrism as a sign of the royal dignity and nobility of Christians. When we are seriously ill or in danger of death, we receive the anointing of the sick for inner and outer healing. And anointing with holy oil is also part of the ordination rite for priests and bishops, as a sign of sharing in the Spirit-filled power of Jesus himself.

Occasionally one has the impression that the "gears" of the church itself are missing such oil. Instead of oil, there seems to be sand in the church's gears. This is why the gears grind, and the vehicle occasionally runs hot. What is missing is the oil of the Holy Spirit. When the Spirit is absent, all the lubricants of external activism are useless. What we need above all is the glow, strength, and energy, the luster and the joy of God's Holy Spirit.

May the holy oil be a sign and impetus for us to remember that we have been anointed with the Holy Spirit for the salvation and healing of the world.

The Spirit Who Brings Life (Celebration of Confirmation: John 16:5–7, 12–13)

"It is to your advantage that I go away, for if I do not go away, the Advocate [the Spirit whom the Father sends] will not come to you" (John 16:7). Among the basic truths of salvation, history is that God often sends his people out into the desert, where so much must be left behind. For the desert is the place of renewal, the place of a particularly liberating and saving presence of God. Going into the desert: doesn't that ask us to leave behind our illusions, our false triumphalism?

What is decisive is the presence of God in the Holy Spirit. The fundamental message of both the Old and New Testaments is this: Do not be afraid; I am here, I am with you, you are my people and I am your God. God promises always to be with us. Therefore, fear and excitement are not necessarily signs of faith: those who believe will not buy into all the apocalyptic invocations about the imminent destruction of our church. God's Spirit is here; we can trust in that.

What is this Spirit's message to us? John's Gospel calls him the "Spirit of truth" (John 16:13). Truth is not simply a mood or an emotion, however much these have their place in faith. It is more than this because faith makes a claim on the whole, undivided human being. And a human being is more than a mood or emotion.

In our time, we also have to beware of the irrationalism that seems to be arising. For the Spirit of truth is not a matter of whatever view is currently popular or the majority view in the polls. Biblically, truth is a matter of faithfulness. That is why we hear, The Spirit will "remind you of all that I have said to you" (John 14:26). The Spirit will do nothing, absolutely nothing, only from himself. Remembering and preserving are important words in the New Testament. The Spirit does not simply throw anything overboard, so to speak, to make the boat lighter and deliver it from the waves. The Spirit is not creating a new and different church, but a renewed church—a new way of being this one and only church. The Spirit brings us back to what Christ told us; the Spirit leads us back to the source, to the Sacred Scriptures. This is the experience of the Spirit in the universal church in our day. Only when we take hold of the scriptures and read them together in the community, only when we "share the scriptures" together can the Spirit—often in astonishing ways—set something in motion.

The Spirit encourages us to recall the great testimonies of Scripture and Tradition. Do we even know the wealth we have here, what treasures lie buried here? Are we aware that many criticize a tradition they do not really know anymore? The Spirit of God is a prophetic Spirit. The Spirit speaks into our situations and interprets them, sheds light on them and lays bare what is truly present.

Taking our cue from John's Gospel (see John 16:5–15), we can say, The Spirit reveals to us our transgressions and shortcomings, the narrowness and constrictions in our lives, in order to give us the fullness of life, life from the fullness of God. So, this Spirit is the Spirit of universal dialogue, even critical dialogue. The Spirit situates us and God's church in the midst of the conflicts of the present, making the gospel message actual here and now. The Spirit frees us from fixating on our narrow present situation, opens up new perspectives, and gives us hope. At the same time, this Spirit is a healing force for the injuries and wounds that so many of us carry around today. We must rediscover and make fruitful this prophetic and therapeutic dimension of faith, so that we can also rediscover the actuality of the Spirit who leads us into the fullness of truth.

Celebrating the Eucharist (Reflection on the Eucharist)

The source and summit of our Christian life is the celebration of the Sunday Eucharist.[2] Indeed, is the Eucharist anything less than the celebration of our faith? The Eucharist is not just a private devotion and personal reflection; nor is it merely an instruction in and explanation of faith. Certainly, all this has its place in worship. But what is decisive in the Eucharist is praising and glorifying God, thanking God, worshiping and calling out to God as Lord and giver of all good gifts, and asking for God's mercy. In brief, the Sunday Eucharist is our festive recommitment of ourselves to our Christian faith in God, the Creator, Sustainer, and Redeemer of the world. The Sunday Eucharist is our celebration of God as our God, present with us in the midst of our lives.

Music is central to such a festive recommitment to and celebration of faith. What Paul writes to the Colossians applies to our celebration of the Eucharist: "With gratitude in your hearts sing psalms, hymns and spiritual songs to God" (Col 3:16).

Nature religions have long known that worship and music are inextricably related. The Psalms of the Old Testament knew this, too. It is not a mere coincidence that the Psalter culminates in these verses:

> Alleluia! Praise the LORD!
> Praise God in his sanctuary;
> praise him in his mighty firmament!...
> Praise God with trumpet sound;
> praise him with lute and harp!
> Praise him with tambourine and dance;
> Praise him with strings and pipe!
> Praise God with clanging cymbals,
> Praise him with loud clashing cymbals!
> Let everything that breathes praise the LORD!
> Alleluia!
>
> (Ps 150)

Jesus was part of this tradition. He prayed and sang the psalms. The Gospels tell us that after singing a hymn at the end of the Last Supper, he went out to the Mount of Olives (see Matt 26:30). And of the young church in Jerusalem, we are told that they came together for the breaking of bread and singing songs of praise (see Acts 2:42–47).

The whole of Christian life should be a liturgy, a Eucharist—that is, a life of gratitude. It should be a coming together in the assembly of worship to receive strength and energy to return to everyday life. This is what it means to say that the Eucharist is the source and summit of the whole Christian life.

Feasts and festivals are human in a primal sense. For it is in feasts and festivals that we celebrate the conviction that our lives are held and sustained by a deeper and more comprehensive reality, by an ultimate mystery that we call God in the language of the religion. In Christian liturgy we celebrate that, in Jesus Christ, God has shown himself to be our God, a God of human beings who saves and frees us and calls us to eternal life with him. Liturgy is not about what we should and must do; rather, in liturgy we celebrate with joy and gratitude what God has done for us. It is there that we recall the mighty acts of God in the history of salvation.

But even more than this: in the liturgy God is present in our midst through Jesus Christ in the power of the Holy Spirit; there we get a foretaste of our destination, the fullness of the coming reign of God. In the liturgy, something of the glory of heaven and of the eternal song of the heavenly liturgy breaks into our world here and now: "Holy, holy, holy." Liturgy is an interruption of everyday life. In our era, in particular, do we not need this deeper dimension, these traces and signs of heaven on earth, so that our lives do not become trivial and monotonous? Yes, we need the festive celebration of the Eucharist and its splendor.

For that same reason, we need church music. For, more than any other art, music brings to our consciousness the harmony pervading the cosmos; it gives voice to the longing of human hearts for eternity. But it also expresses the grief and mourning that often befall us in this world. It consoles us and gives us confidence for living. It is a spark of hope for lasting reconciliation in our unreconciled and unpeaceful world. Music is thus a singular experience of *Sursum corda*, of "lift up your hearts."[3] It enfolds us in the all-embracing and all-encompassing mystery of the divine; it is an inkling and taste of our true vocation.

In the ninth book of his *Confessions*, St. Augustine describes his experience in attending a Eucharist being celebrated at St. Ambrose's cathedral church in Milan:

> How I wept during your hymns and songs! I was deeply moved by the music of the sweet chants of your Church. The sounds flowed into my ears and the truth was distilled into my heart. This caused feelings of devotion to overflow. Tears ran, and it was good for me to have that experience.[4]

I WILL GO TO THE ALTAR OF GOD (REFLECTION ON THE EUCHARIST)

The altar has been an image of Jesus Christ since ancient times. He is the foundation and cornerstone on which everything rests and that holds everything together. We all know how important it is in life to have firm ground underfoot, to have points of reference and orientation. The distress that many people suffer in our day consists precisely in the absence of this ground and orientation. So, they fall into fear and panic; they walk directionless as if lost in fog. As Christians, we know upon whom we can build and where we can find our orientation: on Jesus Christ. No one can lay any other foundation (see 1 Cor 3:11)!

Jesus Christ remains present in his church. He is the center and reference point of every community. In the Eucharist, Jesus's death and resurrection become present to us as the ground and goal of our life.

That is why the altar is the reference point for us, the intersection of all our operating systems, so to speak. When we gather around the altar, we recognize that our life is received from Christ, that we are founded on him and find our orientation in him. Likewise, it is from the altar that we are sent out—into our families, into the community, to our places of work and recreation, and out to political life to take responsibility for our society. The altar brings together all that should unfold in the rest of our lives.

Thus, the altar is also a call to us. If we gather here to celebrate the sacrifice of Christ, then it should have consequences in our life.

God accepts us without condition, knowing our weaknesses, our inner distress and limitations. Isn't it true that today human beings are seeking a place where they are accepted, a community that does not value productivity and activism above all? We have life as a gift from God. Let us not, then, forget gratitude and let us present our concerns and needs before God. I mean that it is both our privilege and our duty as Christians to draw regular orientation for our lives from the altar. So, gathering regularly around the altar at Sunday Eucharist is no mere "offer" provided to us, something to be treated like a special offer at a department store where we search for what is cheapest and most pleasing. Sunday Eucharist is much more a "necessity" of life, if our lives are to be truly happy.[5] Celebrating the Eucharist should, then, be the source and summit of our own Christian lives.

But, the Eucharist is also a mandate for building a civilization of love that transforms our world. By baptism and confirmation, every single one of us is called to carry the redeeming and healing communion of Jesus Christ from the altar out into the world. We are to be missionaries sharing with others the great gifts that we have been given. For the world needs our witness to the merciful love of God.

BREAD FOR THE LIFE OF THE WORLD (REFLECTION ON THE EUCHARIST)

Jesus Christ reveals himself as the one sent by God the Father, the origin and goal of all life, in order to still this great hunger of ours: "This is the bread that comes down from heaven. Whoever eats of this bread will live forever" (see John 6:51). Jesus himself is bread for the life of the world. He is the way, the truth, and the life.

Beyond the daily bread, we need to live. Jesus gives us orientation and perspective for our lives through his word. And within the muddle of so many words in our world, what do we need more than light and direction, signposts on which we can rely and build our lives? The word of Jesus truly is bread for our life in the world.

But God wants the whole human being, and so is not present to us only through words. God is also present to us through bodily signs. In the form of bread and wine, Jesus himself is the food he gives to us. In the form of bread and wine, we receive his sacred body and his healing blood as food and drink for the life of the world.

Therefore, let us make the Eucharist ever more the center of our lives, and let us make our whole lives a form of worship. Let us learn anew a stance of reverence and worship. When these are lost, our lives become sick, our world becomes hollow and empty. Precisely now in our time, don't we need to be renewed and strengthened by this bread for the life of the world? Don't all of us have reason to rediscover the Eucharist as the source and summit of our lives?

In the celebration of the Eucharist, when we offer bread and wine as gifts of creation and call God's Holy Spirit down upon them so that they become the body and blood of our Lord Jesus Christ, then something happens for all of creation. The eucharistic transformation anticipates the cosmic transformation of our whole world. For in the end, all of nature, indeed the entire cosmos is to be included in the new creation in which God is all in all. Therefore, the Eucharist is no private matter of every single one of us alone; it is a public sign and testimony, an anticipatory celebration of the reign of God that one day will embrace all of reality together.

FAMILY AS THE SOURCE OF LIFE (REFLECTION ON MARRIAGE)

Families are the source of life for the church, just as they are for the state. Families are the vital cell of life. From the very beginning of creation, God provided for marriage and the family. God willed that the source of new life should be in the mutual love of woman and man. God wants us to be cocreators in passing on life, and so created us in God's own image. And since God is Love, God created us human beings for love. Only persons who experience love and share love find happiness and fulfillment in their own lives; only they can become the source of life for others. According to God's will, the concrete place for this is normally in the partnership of marriage and in family life.

Many believe that marriage and family are outmoded institutions, that they are an outdated model. They would like to replace these institutions with so-called alternative communities of life. But we cannot simply overturn the reality of

God's creation. Sooner or later human nature will have its say and insist on being heard. Indeed, it has long been time for a rethinking. And, if we are to believe public opinion polls, then the large majority of young people, when asked about their view of what happy life looks like, describe a lifelong partnership and the presence of children. This is how God has created us. This is what the state should protect and promote. Anything else infringes on God's order of creation and on human beings' desire for happiness.

Families are the basic cell of societies and nations. Families are places in which we learn what we so deeply need later in life: open doors, that is, mutual consideration, solidarity, and willingness to lend a hand. If these fundamental practices are not learned and practiced in families, then we will have regrettable outbursts of violence, some of which we are already seeing. The family is the cradle and school of culture and of social behavior. It is the source of life for nations.

Life in the family is no dreamland and no island of blessedness. We must see family life realistically as a place of manifold everyday conflicts. Partnerships of love are a great ideal and clearly also a great thing, though we know also that many are failing in our day. Marriage and family life are not some garden of paradise; too often they are a desert where persons are overcome with thirst. This is a tragedy—certainly for the partners, but also for the children and for our whole society. Marriage partnerships need to be lived day to day in mutual respect, tolerance, and patience; they must always reopen themselves to conversation and must demonstrate their integrity again and again. Each day these partnerships face new challenges.

Only those who draw on and live from deep sources in their own lives can be a source of life for others. The real tragedy is that we too often forget about God, the primal source of all life, and so threaten to dry up in thirst. This is the call of

Jesus: "Let anyone who is thirsty come to me, and let the one who believes in me drink" (John 7:37–38).

Only if we know our good Father in heaven and orient ourselves on him and his image; only if we know that we and others are accepted and borne up by God; only if we know that we are held up by him in good and bad days alike; only if we live consciously with and from God; only then will we have the strength to endure in the kind of life God wants from us and that is best for us, even in the midst of the difficulties and crises that are part of every marriage and family.

BEING CALLED (REFLECTION ON VOCATION)

Every human being and especially every Christian is a person called by God. All of us exist only because God wants us to be and has called us by name. But wherever we look in the Old and New Testaments alike, we also see that God has called individual human beings in particular ways in every age to serve their own people and others.

This begins with Abraham, our forerunner in faith, whom God called forth "from hearth and home"—sending Abraham out toward a land he did not know and making him the forefather of God's people. These vocation stories continue with the other patriarchs, and with Samuel and the equally young David. They go further with the prophets: Amos, Isaiah, Jeremiah, Ezekiel, and many more.

Jesus, too, did not call the people of Israel in general to conversion and to faith in the coming reign of God. Instead he called individual disciples by name into a particular relationship with him, "to be with him, and to be sent out" (Mark 3:14). It saddened him that the crowds seemed like sheep without a shepherd, disoriented (see Matt 9:36). So, he chose shepherds to succeed him and to be good shepherds in his image—that is, to be shepherds who would lay down their lives and hand them over so others would have life in its fullness (see John 10:10–11).

Vocation has been part of the church since the very beginning. The entire history of the church has been a single history of vocation. Over and over again, in all ages, God has called particular women and men. We see this in the lives of all the saints and of all those who have brought new energy to the church, renewing it from within. Vocations arise especially in difficult times in which God needs human beings willing to jump in for the sake of others. Vocations arise wherever the church is truly alive.

In faith, we may be confident that God never leaves his people without vocations. The only issue is whether God's call will be heard, whether we will be open to it and let it in. Often those who are called must first struggle with God before they are ready and can say, "Here I am, Lord; send me" (see Isa 6:8). For they are unexpectedly called out of their normal everyday life. They seem strange to their contemporaries and experience resistance. But woe to us if we no longer have such people willing to show others the way, the truth, and the life—in season or out of season.

We need shepherds who not only show us this way of truth and life, but who themselves live it—with and for others. This is what reaches and convinces others. For love alone is believable. No one has greater love than to lay down one's life for one's friends (see John 15:13).

We must make room in our lives for silence and reflection. We live in a culture of distraction and multiplicity, of the rapidly changing "special offer," and of the conquest of fast food. We are in danger of losing a feeling for the deep mystery of life. All of this can leave us anxious, without orientation, and with a sense of inner emptiness.

We must make room for Jesus Christ, for he is the new

human being. In him, God has shown us concretely who we are as human beings, what our worth and human dignity consist in, what we are called to, and thus what the meaning and mission of our human existence is. God's Spirit is the Spirit of Jesus; this Spirit wants to let Jesus Christ take shape in us and in our world.

Vocation consists in following Jesus, in being called into communion and friendship with him. Jesus does not force anyone into this; but he invites us, just as he invited the first disciples: "Come and see" (John 1:39). He walks along with us, as he did with the disciples at Emmaus; he opens to us the meaning of the scriptures and thus also the meaning of our lives (see Luke 24:13–35). We discover and clarify our vocation by accepting Jesus's invitation for us to be with him, to be accompanied by him, to let him show us the deeper meaning of our life. Vocations arise and mature when we engage the words of Jesus, especially in Scripture, and when we encounter him in the sacraments. Most deeply, vocations mature only in an attitude of prayer.

We must make room for hope. Easter is God's final vindication of hope. Easter has shown us that this hope is stronger than all fear and doubt; it is even stronger than death. It outlasts and conquers all the powers of this world. Hope will be proven right. The Spirit of God, promised to remain in the church for all time, is this hope's guarantor. We would be much worse off—indeed, we would cease to be Christians— were we ever to give up on this hope.

THE GOOD SHEPHERD (MASS OF ORDINATION TO HOLY ORDERS: JOHN 10:11–16)

Those whom we call government deputies and ministers today were referred to as shepherds in the Old Testament.

These shepherds were the great chiefs, the leaders of the clan and of the people. They led their "flock" to good pastures, and thus had authority and rich experience in dealing with men and women and were recognized as such. The Old Testament also knew about the kind of shepherds who only brought their sheep in out of the cold, so to speak, who only filled their own pockets. The prophet Ezekiel engaged in harsh polemics against such shepherds, those who only fed themselves, who fattened up only themselves, who filled only their own pockets. Against this image, Jesus now says, "I am the good shepherd" (John 10:11), the one who really takes responsibility for the flock, for all human beings, the one who does not turn and run when danger threatens; no, I am the one who at the decisive moment gives over his life for those entrusted to him, the one who searches out every single person lost and caught in the thorns, taking that one on my shoulder and returning him to the others. He is not concerned about his own property, but gives all he has for the sake of others. In saying "I am the good shepherd," Jesus wanted to demonstrate the real alternative. He pointed to himself and said, I am the guide and the way; I am a companion and friend for you, the shepherd who carries you, each one individually, who cares for and stands by her, who heals and helps him.

We have such a shepherd, one who is both the guide and the way, one whom we can follow as our shining example. Where else should we go? Where else can we find a model like our model Jesus, one who can show us the way to life, the way to real abundance, to a rich and full life?

And Jesus needs people who, following him, can be shepherds for his people. In his own day, he gathered disciples around himself, both so that they could be with him and so he could send them out. During his own lifetime, he could not go out to all the people who wanted to see him. He needed helpers whom he sent out so they could be shepherds of the people for him and in his place. After his resurrection, he sent out the Twelve in a special way into the whole world, to witness to all peoples the good news of God, of the living God in whom we have life, of the God who is a friend of life. They were to act in his name and in his manner. They were not to act in the way of the bad shepherds, but to be an alternative to a society of egoism and "me first." They were to give perspective and hope, to shine a light, to bring consoling warmth, simply because their task was to announce the Easter message of God's commitment to life, to justice, to love; to announce life's victory over the power of death, of injustice, of hatred and violence. Because they were to express God's option for the poor and the weak, they were to take responsibility for others so they, too, could find life, meaning, a way to fulfillment, and to the fullness of life.

Salvation, grace, and hope are given as gifts; they are given from above and beyond us. So a priest, sent into a church and not simply coming from that church, stands as a sign, so to speak, that all of this is a divine promise, pledge, and gift. The priest is to represent Christ, the one who lived fully with and among people. The priest should be Christ among other Christians: one who should always remind us of the vision of the reign of God, the reign of life and of love, righteousness, and holiness. The priest must see to it that this vision of the gospel, of the reign of God, does not perish among the other trends and interests, ideologies and dreams of this world. Priests who live from the gospel and from Jesus Christ and who accompany others on this way, who are shepherds in the manner and spirit and image of Jesus Christ, are a grace, a gift for the church: a gift that we are not able simply to make happen or establish, a grace for which we can only ask, for which we can only pray.

Deacons and Priests
(Reflection on Ordination)

"Be like those who are waiting for their master to return from the wedding banquet" (Luke 12:36). Be awake, pray, be ready—these are fundamental words of ordained life. These words express what is particularly important: living in light of eternity. The temporal takes a step back. One thing becomes essential: a focused and faithful attentiveness to nothing less than God—for God alone is sufficient.

Weddings and wedding banquets are used frequently in Scripture as images for eternity, toward which everything flows. These two images tell us that eternity in the presence of God and in intimate communion with God is no boring infinite progression of time. It is "high time," because it is one single celebration of joy, a gift of unending love; it is *kairos*, because it is life in its fullness, completely fulfilled life. Jesus Christ came into the world in order to give us this fullness of life (see John 10:10). Our Master, Jesus Christ, has gone ahead of us to the wedding banquet; in the end, he will bring us home to himself there.

This wedding banquet happens, now in our midst, every time we celebrate the Eucharist. Each time we celebrate the Eucharist, the heavens open and bring our life in time and space to the heavenly banquet hall; heaven bows down to share its joy with us here and now. We are invited to join the angels and saints in praising and giving thanks to God, and so to share in divine life, love, friendship, and communion already here and now.

It is noteworthy that the service of both deacons and priests is connected to the Last Supper, where Jesus looked ahead to the heavenly banquet (see Luke 22:17–18). The diaconate is connected to the washing of feet: in this action Jesus wanted to give us a sign of his own self-giving service, and at the same time to ask us to do what he has done (John 13:15). And Jesus refers to the priesthood in saying, "Do this in remembrance of me" (Luke 22:19).

The service of both deacons and priests is thus grounded in the Last Supper, and is ordered to the heavenly wedding banquet made present in the eucharistic meal. The deacon is to bring bread and wine, "fruit of the earth and work of human hands," to the altar to become the body and blood of Jesus Christ. The deacon is equally to share this sacred body and blood as food and drink for eternal life: in these gifts, our earth and our own lives are brought to God to be transformed. The priest acts in the Eucharist, through the authority given in ordination and in the name of Jesus Christ and the power of the Holy Spirit, to transform the bread and wine into the body and blood of Christ; he does this so that we may take part in the heavenly banquet with and in Jesus Christ already now, so that we may celebrate the feast of all eternity already here and now in our earthly lives.

Messengers of Christ (Reflection on Ordination)

"Hear, O Israel: The Lord is our God, the Lord alone" (Deut 6:4). We are to live for God with all our soul and all our mind and all our strength (see Mark 12:30). Undivided service for God and God's reign, indeed passion for God and God's reign, a passion that leads one to set everything else aside and put all one's eggs in one basket, so to speak: this is the motive and foundation of priestly existence.

God is the one and only God. God alone can truly help us, save us, fulfill us, and make us happy. We must be converted to God, returning to God with all our soul, all our mind, and all our strength. And so, we need people who not only tell us this but live it; we need people who make the message of God and God's reign their profession, indeed, who make it the content of their whole life.

As messengers of Christ, priests take on the ministry of reconciliation. What could be more important than working for peace and reconciliation—when there is so much violence, so much hatred and strife, so much egoism in the world; when there are brutal wars, when so much that is unreconciled lies within us ourselves, and when even in our churches and communities there is so much disquiet and suspicion, polarization, such a lack of dialogue and communication? For, what do we human beings long for more than for peace and reconciliation?

To be a messenger of Christ and to be able to work as Jesus worked, a priest must seek on a daily basis to be in friendship and communion with Jesus Christ. Without him we can do nothing (see John 15:5).

Daily celebration of the Eucharist is to be the center of the priest's life. God does not compel us, but makes possible what he wants from us. So, let us remind ourselves that we do not "make" the church, that we do not "make" peace. If it were so, it would be impossible. But Jesus says, "All authority in heaven and on earth has been given to me" (Matt 28:18). That means be assured that the church is no leaky ship about to sink. The church will survive all storms.

Priests of this church are witnesses of hope, a hope for peace and reconciliation, for justice and for life. At the beginning, there were only eleven, and those eleven changed the world.

Priests are witnesses of hope, messengers of joy. As a priest, your joy will be infectious; it will console, encourage, and strengthen others. It will be convincing.

To be a teacher in our day is no easy task. People frequently do not want to hear talk of truth; often, they seek teachers according to their own taste. They seek teachers who suit their own desires and tell them what they want to hear (see 2 Tim 4:3). Too often they do not want to hear what Jesus asks of us. They find it all disdainful, even ridiculous, and set it aside. But we should be sure of this: the word of Jesus lasts until the end of time. "Jesus Christ is the same yesterday and today and forever" (Heb 13:8). Right now, in our own day, he remains the way, the truth, and the life (John 14:6).

Priestly Life

People need and want priests who can interpret the Word of God for them, share eucharistic bread with them, accompany them on their life's way, share a ministry of reconciliation with them, and be their brother, friend, and pastor in the community of the church. Young people, especially, are seeking priests who are partners with them.

"Ask the Lord of the harvest to send out laborers into his harvest" (Matt 9:38). Whoever asks anything in Jesus's name will be given it by the Father (see John 16:23). God has made the calling and sending of workers into the vineyard a matter of God's own concern. God is directly concerned with it, but has also made it a matter of our concern through our prayer. One cannot make priestly vocations happen, and one cannot simply demand them with a loud voice. They are a gift and the fruit of prayer. But do we pray enough for them? Are we truly convinced of the power of such prayer?

"Jesus went about all the cities and villages, teaching in their synagogues, and proclaiming the good news of the kingdom, and curing every disease and every sickness" (Matt 9:35). But then the question arises: How does this continue after Jesus? In response, what follows in the Gospel is the great missionary discourse: the commissioning of the Twelve, the instructions for mission, and the call for a fearless confession of faith (see Matt 10).

What stands out in Matthew's missionary discourse is that the power and authority with which Jesus taught and healed is henceforth passed on to the Twelve, but also that the attitude and destiny of Jesus is to become the attitude and destiny of the Twelve. Like Jesus, they are to be poor and without defenses, and they are to reckon with opposition, rejection, and persecution. They are sent like sheep into the midst of wolves. But, also like Jesus, they are sent out under the care of God: "Do not worry" and "Have no fear of them" (see Matt 10:19, 26). Like Jesus the Good Shepherd, the disciples are to hand over their life. For "those who find their life will lose it, and those who lose their life for my sake will find it" (Matt 10:39). In and through his disciples, Jesus continues to speak, work, suffer, and live in history. So, it is true: "Whoever welcomes you welcomes me, and whoever welcomes me welcomes the one who sent me" (Matt 10:40). This is how the missionary discourse concludes.

The model for who priests are to be is thus clear for all time. Being human, becoming more human, being open to human formation are the first and most fundamental prerequisites for the ministry of priests. No great official authority, no high theology, and no wonderful pastoral method matters without a humanly formed heart; none of it matters if kindness, sincerity, fairness, and reliability are lacking, or if the priest is not reliable and open, if the priest is not humble enough to be a believable witness.

Jesus continues to speak and work through his disciples; he remains present in and through his church, to which he promised his lasting presence (see Matt 28:20). Certainly, we must distinguish between Jesus and the church, but we must never separate one from the other. There is much to criticize about the church as it exists, everyone knows this.

But only one who himself has left Jesus behind could say that the church has departed from Jesus. For one reads in Scripture that Jesus loves the church and gave his life for it (see Eph 5:25). One may not become a priest if one does not love the church; in fact, one may not call oneself a Christian without loving the church. Therefore, it is our fundamental task to grow in the church as it exists and to get to know it, so that with and through it we can learn to find and love Jesus Christ.

Monastic Life

A monk is someone who seeks and loves God above all else. In his monastic rule, St. Benedict (480–547) writes that if a newcomer, a novice, wants to enter the monastery, then one should check to see whether the person is seeking God. In describing monastic life, Benedict writes about what is most important: "In the first place, to love the Lord God with the whole heart, the whole soul, the whole strength."[6] Monastic life, then, is not at all something extraordinary or enigmatic; it is about fulfilling Jesus's first commandment about loving God in all things and above all things, preferring God to all other things—even to the best of things, like marriage and family life. So, in the rule of Benedict, nothing can come before worship.

Monks, therefore, want to take God's existence seriously, taking absolutely seriously that God is the truest, final, deepest, all-pervading, and all-surpassing reality. They want to live so as to show that, in the end, our life can find meaning and fulfillment only from, in, and through God. Swiss theologian Walter Nigg has written, "The monk is the religious human being par excellence…and thus also a pioneer, one who does not only preach a path to others, but walks it him- or herself."[7]

Not least, but the most mature of our contemporaries are those who perceive the inner emptiness into which we have fallen, and once again sense the spiritual longing that is in us as human beings. Therefore, we need to relearn reverence for the mystery of God; we need to bow down before God in prayer. We need places and times for silence and reflection, so that we can develop a sense of God as the deep, incomprehensible, and yet wonderful, consoling, and blissful mystery in and beyond our lives. Something of the secluded life of the monk is necessary for all of us if we are to become capable of finding God in all things in the midst of daily life and thus of retrieving a sense of the meaning and purpose, of the foundation and substance of our lives. In short, we must become more prayerful human beings.

A monk is one who takes Jesus's call to discipleship completely seriously and strives to follow Jesus Christ in a radical way. It is not an accident that the first word of the rule of St. Benedict is *obsculta,* "listen." And the first biblical text cited in the rule is from the thirteenth chapter of Paul's Letter to the Romans: "Now is the moment for you to wake from sleep" (Rom 13:11). Indeed, from the very beginning, a crucial role of monasticism was to shake and awaken a Christendom that had grown rather drowsy. The first monks refused to be satisfied with a bourgeois and secularized Christian existence. They wanted to take very seriously that Jesus himself lived a poor, unmarried, and obedient life.

Monasticism was and remains a salutary reminder of the call of Jesus. Theologian Johannes Metz writes, "Religious orders are a kind of shock therapy introduced by the Holy Spirit for the church as a whole."[8] We, too, must hear again Jesus's call to us to follow him; we must rise from our sleep. We need young women and men who are inspired to devote themselves entirely and unreservedly to following Jesus, who take up the ideals of monasticism and thus hold out a light to others in the darkness, giving them signposts for the way.

The first monks knew that living for God by following Jesus was possible only in the power and grace of the Holy Spirit. In the prologue of his rule, St. Benedict writes that we cannot achieve any of this with our own strength and thus must pray for the help of grace. In another place he writes that a life of virtue can be joyful rather than a burden and an affliction only through the Holy Spirit.

We can also learn from monks what Christian life in the world looks like: God must more and more become the center of life in our day-to-day lives in the world. Precisely in the confusion of our day, we must orient ourselves on Jesus in a more determined way and allow him to be the measure of our lives. We must learn again to trust in the Holy Spirit and in the Spirit's merciful work, so that we may live and act as Christians in this world of ours.

CHAPTER EIGHT

SACRED MUSIC— CHURCH MUSIC

MUSIC—SIGN OF HOPE

Church music and liturgy form an inner unity, for the liturgy is essentially dependent on church music. A liturgical celebration in which nothing was sung would be missing an essential element, and anyone who sees church music as nothing more than a decorative accessory underestimates its value.

"Hope rises like a song."[1] This statement suggests something of the inner connection between liturgy and music; it suggests an answer to the question of why church music exists at all and why it is so important to the church. The key word here is "hope."

People with hope see something that those without hope do not see. They see beyond what is given. They see a light on the horizon of even the greatest darkness—a light that leads them on their way and strengthens them with courage. Hope is not only crucial for us when we find ourselves in a desperate situation. In the end, everything we do and even imagine is supported by some hope. We hope that we can finish well what we have started, or we hope that we can turn an idea into reality. When we get out of bed in the morning, we begin the day with the hope that it will turn out well. When we lie down at night to sleep, we trust in hope that we will wake again in the morning.

Human beings are creatures of hope, and in hope we transcend ourselves. For by hoping we step beyond our current situation and are present to what is not yet. Ultimately, true hope always aims at the absolute. Thus, hope finds its lasting fulfillment only in God. As creatures of hope, we human beings can only be completely ourselves in God. God alone can be the answer to the question that we ourselves are.

The meaning of hope finds unique expression in music. For music allows our human longing for the absolute to come to expression in a very special way. It is the most spiritual of all the arts. It appeals most directly to our hearts. A contemporary philosopher once called music "a mirror of hope."[2] Another contemporary philosopher who made hope the center of his thinking has written, "Music shows that there is a seed, no more, but no less, which could blossom into eternal joy and continue on in the darkness."[3]

Christian faith gives human hope a foundation, a goal, and a name: Jesus Christ. Faith places things in relation to God and thus allows them to be seen in a different light. Through faith in Jesus Christ our life receives a goal and thus a direction, so that we can say with Paul, "We boast in our hope of sharing the glory of God" (Rom 5:2).

This is the wonderful thing: that future glory does not appear apart from our life, but in the midst of our life, in the midst of our weakness and infirmity. So, we may rejoice. So, festivity and ceremony are essential elements of liturgy. So, music and liturgy together form an inner coherence. Music expresses what is most deeply happening in liturgy. Church music is an inner and sensuous expression of our Christian hope in the final coming of Jesus Christ. It is also a prelude to the heavenly songs of praise that will be heard when God is all in all. It is not at all an accident that, in the Book of Revelation, the visionary John portrays human beings in their fulfillment with God as singing and playing music (see Rev 14:2–3).

THE SINGING JESUS

We see the theological foundation for church music in the gospel accounts of the Last Supper and of Jesus's going out to the Mount of Olives. The evangelist Mark tells us, "When they had sung the hymn, they went out to the Mount of Olives" (Mark 14:26). Thus, Jesus not only prayed the psalm; he sang it with his disciples. Unfortunately, theology has reflected little on the singing Jesus. Had it done so, we would recognize more deeply our need to treasure and cultivate church music. For church music is nothing less than our joining in with Jesus's own worship of God. In the singing of the eucharistic assembly, Jesus's worship has continued to resound through the centuries in the voices of the Body of Christ, which the church is. Already the New Testament was urging and encouraging us: "With gratitude in your hearts sing psalms, hymns, and spiritual songs to God" (Col 3:16).

Like no other art, music brings to voice the harmony that permeates the cosmos; it brings to voice the longing of the human heart for eternity. At the same time, the laments and mourning that so often fill this world of ours are given expression in music. Again, at the same time, music consoles and encourages us. It is like a spark of hope for the final reconciliation of all that remains unreconciled in our unpeaceful world. It is a singular experience of our liturgical exclamation *sursum corda*, "Lift up your hearts." It enfolds us in the all-embracing and all-encompassing mystery of the divine; it is an inkling and taste of our true vocation.

As the most spiritual of the arts, music must break us out of the danger of mediocrity. It should remind us again and again that we human beings are more than we may think, that we are called to freedom and eternal life.

Church music is an expression of who we already are as Christians, but it is also help for us in fulfilling our Christian mission in the world. Christian art has always been an important bridge between church and world; it has been a crucial means of reaching human hearts and of attracting those who stand outside the visible church. It speaks a language that reaches into the hearts of even those who no longer understand our explicitly theological language.

Music not only gives voice to the harmony of the world. It also has healing and reconciling power in all that is still unreconciled in our world.

Music—Bridge to the Heart

Philosopher Theodor Adorno (1903–69) once expressed this insight: "Aesthetic behavior is the ability to perceive more in things than they are."[4] Well put: "more than they are" and not only "more than they seem to be." Art is concerned not only with unmasking external appearances, but also with transcending actual facts themselves. It is concerned with transforming the world in view of a possible future reconciliation. For Adorno, art lives in the discrepancy between what actually is and the truth that should be.

Art is of central importance in the face of the banalization that threatens our lives. In and through art, a transformation of the material realities of this world begins. In and through art, what is missing, or sick, or broken, or hypocritical becomes clear to us. In and through art, the hope for something greater is kept alive. Art is, so to speak, the natural ally of the Christian message. After a long period of estrangement, they both need a renewed friendship with each other.

This is especially true of music. It is the most spiritual of all the arts. It is certainly dependent on instruments, and it engages physical and mathematical laws of vibration and rhythm. But it transforms these materially given realities into a pure sound that not only reaches our ears, but produces vibrations in our hearts as well.

So, music gives voice to the longing of the human heart for eternity. But music also gives voice to the laments and griefs that often befall us in this world. It is able to comfort us and give us fresh courage. It is an expression of joy and exultation; through music, we can praise and thank God for God's miraculous deeds. In this way, music can be an important companion to human beings on our pilgrimage home to ourselves and to God. Music gives us a sense of our true destiny. Music pricks up our ears to listen, pulls us out of the busyness of our everyday life, and can help us find the depths of our being once again.

Music raises claims about truth. Adorno says that it "puts truth back into the picture." It protests against all that is banal and transcends what is merely factual. And thus it speaks to us from the depth of our own hearts.

Aesthetics is gaining in importance in view of the increasing secularization of our culture. For the tones of music can still reach those whom the words of preaching have long been unable to reach. Music can bridge and overcome the schism between faith and life, between faith and culture—a schism that has become the drama of our age. The church, then, depends on music. Music can become a bridge to the hearts of human beings.

Through music, creation can come into tune and harmony here and now; it can lead us toward praising and thanking the Creator. In the music of our liturgical assemblies, the cosmic liturgy has already begun here and now.

CHURCH MUSIC

Church music is more than a decorative adornment to the liturgy. Instead, church music and liturgy form one inner unity. The Second Vatican Council was not afraid to say that sacred music "forms a necessary and integral part of the solemn liturgy" (Constitution on the Sacred Liturgy 112). Liturgy relies on church music in an essential way, and the ministry of church musicians is a liturgical ministry.

This ministry has only grown in importance in our era during which it has become more difficult to pass on faith to the coming generation. Music still reaches many today whom preaching can no longer reach. This is evident in worship experiences with music of high quality; it is also evident in music festivals and concerts featuring works of church music.

Beyond every other art form, music speaks to people in an immediate way. And, again beyond other art forms, music is able to lead us beyond ourselves. It brings us together and can be understood around the whole world, and thus has a universal, interlinking element. Both Theodor Adorno and Arnold Schoenberg spoke about the truth of music.[5] Music can make real to us what goes beyond that which presents itself as factual. Music lets things be seen as more than they factually are. More than any other art, music can awaken us to our human longing for fulfillment and can give us a means for expressing it. Adorno called music a "mirror of hope." And Ernst Bloch, the important philosopher of hope, once said that music is a "pledge from the beyond...the nighttime flower of faith that strengthens us in the final darkness, and the most powerfully transcendent certainty between heaven and earth."[6]

Is that not precisely what unites music and the Christian good news so closely together? For the Christian message is one of hope and of life. It, too, wants to keep alive our longing for final salvation. It, too, wants to keep us from being satisfied with the modest, too often narrow-minded ideas of bourgeois happiness. It wants to lead us beyond all that toward openness to the possibilities that we can receive from God.

We reach new life by way of the cross, through our pains, sufferings, and eventual death. The way passes through the experience of lament: "I have labored in vain, I have spent my strength for nothing and vanity" (Isa 49:4a). This, too, is part of faith. Through music about the passion, church music brings this lament to heartfelt expression. Yet, in the song of the Suffering Servant, lament passes into the praise of God and of God's faithfulness: "Yet surely my cause is with the LORD, and my reward with my God" (see Isa 49:4b). In the resurrection of Jesus, which we celebrate at Easter, God conquered death and obtained life in its fullness for us. Our longing does not die off in dark emptiness. Its fulfillment is already real in the midst of all the brokenness and imperfection; in fact, it has a name: Jesus Christ. The festive Alleluia of Easter applies to him. For through and in him the new dispensation, the reign of God, has already begun.

We give voice to our faithfulness in both the songs of lament of Holy Week and the Alleluia of Easter. We join with all creation in both its songs of lament and of praise. The music that resounds in our worship gives voice to what is happening in the liturgy: it reflects both how lost we are without God's saving grace and how present the salvation granted us in Jesus Christ is.

Sacred Music

Friedrich Nietzsche wrote, "They would have to sing better songs for me to believe in their savior: his disciples would have to look more redeemed!"[7] Better songs and more redeemed-looking disciples could indeed lead us to learn anew our faith in the Savior, or to understand better the faith we have already learned.

The melodies of church music are also able to reach those whom the preached word has long been unable to reach. They can be a hint and a pointer to God.

And so, church music can bridge and do away with the schism between faith and life, between faith and culture. Music can help reconcile church and world. Josef Ratzinger (Pope Benedict XVI) has written, "The Church is to transform, improve, 'humanize' the world—but how can she do that if at the same time she turns her back on beauty, which is so closely allied to love? For together beauty and love form the true consolation in this world, bringing it as near as possible to the world of the resurrection. The church…must be a place where beauty can be at home."[8]

Despite our differences in language, we can all understand music. It essentially transcends nations and time: we can all enjoy music, and no national boundary can long prevent music from uniting cultures and bringing together the hearts of all peoples.

Since *musica sacra* (sacred music) is an expression of faith and the outpouring of hearts filled with the Spirit of God, it can bring into deeper communion all those who love the same Lord and read the same scriptures, a phrase Pope St. John XXIII used to describe all Christians together.

Church music brings about ecumenical bonds. It shows that our divisions do not go to the roots of Christianity. For we learn to sing first with one voice and then with one heart,

197

and so come to understand each other better. Music, not least of all, can help us attain the near goals of ecumenical engagement—namely, that the divisions and poison of hostility be left behind, and our commonwealth of faith be rediscovered. As important as music and its ecumenical unifying powers are, what is most important about it has not yet been mentioned. For *musica sacra* in its deepest dimensions does not only seek to bring human beings together with each other; it seeks to be a bond between God and human beings. Sacred music wants to make every word that comes forth from the mouth of God and is so essential for our lives as human beings into its own word of both heart and speech, and it wants to give that word back to God with praise and thanks, with lament and petition.

Sacred music is so essential to us human beings, who can only live when we are united with and in God. For it is able to penetrate into the deep chambers of our minds and the obscure corners of our hearts. Sacred music reaches to the very foundations where the primal forces of life reach out to us. From the faith in which it is anchored, *musica sacra* can bring consolation to our fears, give expression to our petitions and laments, help us overcome our sufferings with melodies of hope, and let the beauty of our ultimate fulfillment shine forth already now in the midst of the chaos of this world.

Understood in this way, music is a form of prayer—complex, individual, and universal, all at once. It brings our entire humanity before God, along with our pleas for redemption and salvation.

NOTES

CHAPTER 1

1. Heraclitus was a Greek philosopher remembered primarily for his reflections on change.

2. Kasper seems to be referring to the closing paragraphs of Augustine's *The City of God*. In the final chapter of the last book of that volume (that is, Book XXII, chap. 30), Augustine writes that we ourselves are awaiting the perpetual Sabbath of the City of God.

3. I am citing Austin Flannery, ed., *Vatican Council II: The Basic Sixteen Documents, A Completely Revised Translation in Inclusive Language* (Northport, NY: Costello Publishing Company, 1996), here at p. 150. All English translations of conciliar documents cited here are from Flannery's edition.

4. Ancient Greece had two words for time: *chronos* (from which the English word *chronology* comes), meaning "time as passing," and *kairos*, meaning "a moment of great significance," "time out of time," as we might say in English.

5. Scholars do not universally agree that Christians came to celebrate Christmas on December 25 because of that date's connection to the Roman imperial festival day. But the fact that Constantine (272–337) was the first Roman emperor

to claim conversion to Christianity (in 312) lends credence to this view.

6. *Adveniat* is a charitable arm of the German Catholic Church. Its focus is now on helping the poor of Latin America. See http://www.adveniat.org/ (accessed November 6, 2017).

7. A website for Americans who want to understand German customs explains the contemporary tradition of the *Sternsinger*: "Every year between Christmas and Epiphany, hundreds of thousands of German kids travel from house to house singing carols and collecting money for good causes. These kids are known as Sternsinger ('star singers'), and their efforts are part of a Catholic initiative that has been ongoing since 1959. Between December 25 and January 6, these kids dress up in colorful robes, wear gold crowns and carry a star. They represent the three Wise Men (Magi). When they arrive at a Catholic house, they sing carols and bless the house by writing an inscription over the door with a stick of chalk. At the same time, these kids ask for donations for various charities and causes." See http://www.germany.info/Vertretung/usa/en/03-Topics/04-Language-Study-Research/WoW/2016/01-Sternsinger.html (accessed November 6, 2017).

8. Its website describes *Misereor* as "the German Catholic Bishops' Organization for Development Cooperation. For over 50 years *Misereor* has been committed to fighting poverty in Africa, Asia and Latin America. Its support is available to any human being in need—regardless of their religion, ethnicity or gender." See http://www.misereor.org/about-us.html (accessed November 6, 2017).

We know the work of *Bread for the World* in our country. See http://www.bread.org/ (accessed November 6, 2017). And perhaps our nearest equivalent to German Catholics' "fast offerings" is in Catholic Relief Services' Lenten

"Operation Rice Bowl." See http://www.crsricebowl.org/ (accessed November 6, 2017).

9. *Renovabis* is the German Catholic Church's effort to help in the rebuilding and development of Eastern Europe. See https://www.renovabis.de/ (accessed November 6, 2017).

10. Kasper may be thinking of the following sentence from no. 8: "The Church, embracing in its bosom sinners, at the same time holy and always in need of being purified, always follows the way of penance and renewal."

11. By modernism and historicism, Kasper seems to be referring to the late nineteenth and early twentieth centuries' philosophical and cultural tendencies to believe in the inevitability of progress.

12. Kasper seems to be referring to no. 35 of Pope John Paul II's 2001 Apostolic Letter *Novo Millennio Ineunte*: "In the twentieth century, especially since the Council, there has been a great development in the way the Christian community celebrates the Sacraments, especially the Eucharist. It is necessary to continue in this direction, and to stress particularly *the Sunday Eucharist* and *Sunday* itself experienced as a special day of faith, the day of the Risen Lord and of the gift of the Spirit, the true weekly Easter. For two thousand years, Christian time has been measured by the memory of that 'first day of the week' (*Mk* 16:2,9; *Lk* 24:1; *Jn* 20:1), when the Risen Christ gave the Apostles the gift of peace and of the Spirit (cf. *Jn* 20:19–23). The truth of Christ's Resurrection is the original fact upon which Christian faith is based (cf. *1 Cor* 15:14), an event set *at the centre of the mystery of time*, prefiguring the last day when Christ will return in glory. We do not know what the new millennium has in store for us, but we are certain that it is safe in the hands of Christ," see https://w2.vatican.va/content/john-paul-ii/en/apost_letters/

2001/documents/hf_jp-ii_apl_20010106_novo-millennio
-ineunte.html (accessed November 6, 2017).

CHAPTER 2

1. Pope St. Leo the Great, Sermon 21:3. St. Leo
preached this sermon on Christmas Day in the year 440. A
good English translation can be found in St. Leo the Great,
Sermons, FOTC Patristic Series 93, trans. Jane Patricia Free-
land and Agnes Josephine Conway (Washington, DC: The
Catholic University of America Press, 1996), here at 79.

2. Kasper seems to be referring here to a Latin phrase
often attributed to St. Augustine: *Amo, volo ut sis.* "I love
you, I want you to be."

3. This is a literal English rendering of the German text
of the Latin Christmas hymn *Adeste Fideles*. We, of course,
know it by the following words: "O come, all ye faithful, joyful and triumphant, O come ye, O come ye to Bethlehem.
Come and behold Him, born the King of angels...O come let
us adore him...Christ the Lord."

4. St. Augustine, *The Confessions*, Book I:1. The English translation of *The Confessions* cited here is *St. Augustine Confessions*, a new translation by Henry Chadwick
(New York: Oxford University Press, 1991).

5. Kasper is citing the *Commentary of Saint Ambrose
on the Gospel According to Saint Luke*.

6. Kasper is citing a Christmas homily of Karl Rahner.
See Rahner, *The Great Church Year: The Best of Karl
Rahner's Homilies, Sermons, and Meditations*, trans. and
ed. Harvey D. Egan (New York: Crossroad, 1993), 49.

7. This is a more literal rendition of the opening words
of the German Christmas carol. As commonly sung in English,

the words read, "Lo, how a rose e'er blooming from tender stem hath sprung."

8. Catholic Mass texts cited in this volume are taken from: *The Roman Missal: Renewed by Decree of the Most Holy Second Ecumenical Council of the Vatican, Promulgated by Authority of Pope Paul VI and Revised at the Direction of Pope John Paul II* (Collegeville, MN: Liturgical Press, 2011), here at 152.

9. Kasper seems to be referring to the so-called Oslo Accords of fall 1993. At that time, the peace process between Israel and the then Palestine Liberation Organization created the Palestinian Authority and brought limited self-governance over parts of the West Bank and Gaza.

10. The scriptural reference here and in the hymn "Lo, How a Rose E'er Blooming," is to Isaiah, chap. 11.

11. The text above is a more literal translation of the third German verse of the song. In English, that verse is usually rendered:

This flow'r whose fragrance tender
With sweetness fills the air,
Dispels with glorious splendor
The darkness ev'rywhere....
From sin and death He saves us
And lightens ev'ry load.

CHAPTER 3

1. The title of this introduction and of the chapter are, of course, a translation of Kasper's episcopal motto: *Veritatem in caritate.*

2. In his essay *On the Genealogy of Morals* (1887), Nietzsche wrote that Christians are guilty of "the duplicity

of impotence—as though the weakness of the weak, which is after all his essence, his natural way of being, his sole and inevitable reality, were a spontaneous act, a meritorious deed." Friedrich Nietzsche, *The Birth of Tragedy and The Genealogy of Morals*, trans. Francis Golffing (Garden City, NY: Doubleday & Company, 1956), 179–80.

3. Kasper is playing on two German words sharing the same root: *Gabe* (gift) and *Aufgabe* (task or duty).

4. The footnote in the NRSV text of Matthew says at this point: "Jesus' words 'It is I,' can also be translated 'I am,' suggesting the mysterious divine presence (see Exodus 3:14; Isaiah 43:10; John 18:2–9)."

5. The German word for doubt, *Zweifel*, is a compound noun made up of two parts, *zwei* and *Fälle*, "two cases or considerations." To doubt is to be of two minds.

6. There is a beautiful play on words in the German text that is not evident in the English translation. The German word for hard-hearted (*hartherzig*) is contrasted to the German word for merciful (*barmherzig*).

7. Kasper is making reference to the title of Charles Dickens's fairy tale *The Cricket on the Hearth: A Fairy Tale of Home*. At the beginning of Dickens's story, a husband, wife, and their baby live contentedly at home, while a cricket on the hearth acts as their guardian angel.

CHAPTER 4

1. Blaise Pascal (1623–62) was a French mathematician and Christian philosopher and theologian. His book *Pensées* (literally "thoughts") is a collection of fragments of theology and philosophy written in defense of Christianity. The English translation cited here is by W. F. Trotter, *Pascal's*

Pensées, with an introduction by T.S. Eliot (New York: E.P. Dutton & Co., 1958), 142.

2. The immediate gospel text Kasper is referring to seems to be John 4:26, where Jesus responds to the Samaritan woman's declaration of her faith in the coming messiah with these words: "I am, the one who is speaking to you." It is significant that there is no predicate object of the verb. Jesus says simply "I am" here, and seven other times in John's Gospel (8:24, 28, 58; 13:19; 18:5, 6, 8). He uses some version of "I am" forty-five times in John's Gospel. Scripture scholars point out that the meaning of the Hebrew words for God's name in the Old Testament (YHWH) is closely related to "I am" (see Exod 3:14 and many other places).

3. For example, the story of the miracle at Cana ends with these words: "Jesus did this, the first of his signs, in Cana of Galilee, and revealed his glory; and his disciples believed in him" (John 2:11).

4. *Dives in misericordia* ("Rich in Mercy") is the Latin title of the second encyclical written by Pope John Paul II (1980).

5. This is the English Lutheran Hymnal's translation of lyrics from the seventeenth-century German song *O Haupt voll Blut und Wunden.* The song was translated into English as "O sacred head surrounded." It originated in the thirteenth century as the Latin hymn entitled *Salve caput cruentatum.*

6. As the text makes clear, this reflection was first preached as a homily on the Feast of the Sacred Heart, Year B. The Gospel text often used on that day is John 19:31–37, which includes this verse: "…one of the soldiers pierced his side with a spear, and at once blood and water came out."

7. This reflection seems to have originated as a homily for the Feast of Corpus Christi, Year B. The Gospel reading for that day is Mark 14:12–16, 22–26.

8. In his novel of life at Auschwitz, Jewish writer and Holocaust survivor Eli Wiesel tells a similar story. In response to another murder by the SS, one Jewish prisoner calls out, "Where is God?" And Wiesel's character responds, "Where is He? Here He is—He is hanging here on this gallows." Wiesel, *Night*, trans. Marion Wiesel (New York: Farrar, Strauss, Giroux, 1987).

9. The origins of this hymn for Good Friday seem to be in the words of fifteenth-century German theologian Thomas á Kempis's book, *The Imitation of Christ*: "In the cross is salvation, in the cross is life. There is no…hope of everlasting life, but in the cross."

10. Hans Urs von Balthasar, "Gott und das Leid," in *Die Antwort des Glaubens* (Freiburg: Informationszentrum Berufe der Kirche, 1984), 8. (The book does not appear to have been translated into English.)

CHAPTER 5

1. This, of course, is the title that Kasper gave to this volume in its original German edition: *Wer glaubt, zittert nicht*.

2. Kasper seems to be referring to the Chinese philosopher Mencius (372–289 BCE).

3. Kasper is making a reference to a book by Swiss Catholic theologian Hans Urs von Balthasar, *Was dürfen wir hoffen?* (1986). It was translated into English in 1988 as *Dare We Hope That All Men Be Saved? With a Short Discourse on Hell*.

4. Preface I for the Dead, *Roman Missal*, 594.

5. These are two classic German Easter hymns. The first song begins, "Christ has risen from the martyrs all. We shall all be glad." The second begins, "Let us rejoice greatly…

The clouds have disappeared, alleluia, now the sweet ray of sunshine shines, alleluia."

6. These are the first words of a German church hymn, entitled *Komm, Heil'ger Geist, der Leben schafft.*

7. Kasper seems to be referring to John's account of the encounter between the risen Jesus and Mary Magdalene— see John 20:17: "Jesus said to her: 'Do not hold on to me, because I have not yet ascended to the Father.'"

8. Kasper seems to be referring to *The Pastoral Constitution on the Church* 39: "When we have spread on earth the fruits of our nature and our enterprise—human dignity, sisterly and brotherly communion, and freedom—according to the command of the Lord and his Spirit, we will find them once again, cleansed from the stain of sin, illuminated and transfigured, when Christ presents to his Father an eternal and universal kingdom 'of truth and life, a kingdom of holiness and grace, a kingdom of justice, love and peace.'"

CHAPTER 6

1. This hymn "sequence" is sung just before the Gospel acclamation on the Feast of Pentecost. Its Latin text is usually attributed either to Pope Innocent III (1160–1216) or to Stephen Langton, Archbishop of Canterbury (1150–1228).

2. One of the most widely used hymns in the church, *Veni, Creator Spiritus* is attributed to Rabanus Maurus (776–856).

3. The English text used here is a literal translation of the German version of the song's second verse as Kasper cites it. Though the text fits the context of Kasper's reflection, the usual English translation of this verse is actually closer to the Latin original. Here is the usual English translation, by Edward Caswall (1814–78):

O comforter, to Thee we cry,
O heavenly gift of God Most High,
O fount of life and fire of love,
and sweet anointing from above.

CHAPTER 7

1. Kasper is pointing out that the literal meaning of the Greek title *Christos* given to Jesus means "anointed one." The Hebrew word *Mashiach* (messiah) was translated as *Christos* when the Old Testament was translated into Greek.

2. Kasper is referring to Vatican II's Dogmatic Constitution on the Church 11, on the Eucharist as "the source and summit of the Christian life."

3. The *Sursum Corda* (in Latin, literally, "Hearts lifted up") is the opening of the preface of the Eucharistic Prayer in the Christian celebration of the Eucharist, dating back to at least the third century.

4. St. Augustine, *Confessions*, Book IX: 6.

5. There is a play on German words here that is not quite captured in the English. The Eucharist is not an *Angebot*—a special promotion or sale item at a department store; it is a *Gebot*—a necessity or requirement of our lives.

6. *The Rule of Saint Benedict*, trans. Leonard Doyle (Collegeville, MN: The Liturgical Press, 2001), chap. 4.

7. Swiss theologian Walter Nigg (1903–88) was one of the most important religious authors of his time. He published sixty books on saints, angels, pilgrims, and mystics—reaching millions of people. He was a pastor of the Reformed Church. The source of the text cited here has not been found.

8. Johannes Baptist Metz (born 1928) is a German Catholic theologian. The citation here is taken from Metz,

Followers of Christ: The Religious Life of the Church (London: Burns & Oates, 1978), 12.

CHAPTER 8

1. This is a line in a German liturgical hymn entitled "Der Geist des Herrn erfüllt das All." It also seems to be the title of a publication of the German Catholic diocese for which Kasper served as bishop: Diözese Rottenburg-Stuttgart Amt für Kirchenmusik, *Die Hoffnung hebt sich wie ein Lied* (1994).

2. Kasper says it is German philosopher Theodor Adorno who called music a mirror of hope. See note 4 for further information.

3. Kasper is referring to German philosopher Ernst Bloch (1885–1977), and seems to be referring to a long section of Bloch's masterwork, *The Principle of Hope*, which was republished as *Essays on the Philosophy of Music*. Though I cannot find the precise text cited above, in this work Bloch does call music an "essentially Christian art… becoming the source-sound of self-shapings still unachieved in the world." Bloch, *Essays on the Philosophy of Music*, trans. Peter Palmer (Cambridge, UK: Cambridge University Press, 1985), 219.

4. Adorno was a German philosopher who also composed music. In his book *Aesthetic Theory*, Adorno contrasts aesthetic behavior with what he calls "practical, appetitive behavior." See Adorno, *Aesthetic Theory* (New York: Bloomsbury Academic, 2013), 13.

5. Schoenberg (1874–1951) was an Austrian composer who spent the last decade and a half of his life in the United States.

6. Bloch, *The Spirit of Utopia* (Redwood City, CA: Stanford University Press, 2000), 57.

7. Nietzsche, *Thus Spoke Zarathustra: A Book for Everyone and No One*, chap. 37, "Of the Priests," trans. R. J. Hollingdale (New York: Penguin Books, 1969), 116.

8. Josef Ratzinger (Pope Benedict XVI), *Feast of Faith* (San Francisco: Ignatius Press, 1986), 126.